海南省哲学社会科学 2016 年规划课题成果

[HNSK （ZC） 16—20]

海南师范大学学术著作出版资助项目

（项目号：ZZ1906）

海南旅游与文化概览

A Panoramic View of Hainan Tourism and Culture

吴文姝　杨蕾达　著

暨南大學出版社
JINAN UNIVERSITY PRESS

中国·广州

图书在版编目（CIP）数据

海南旅游与文化概览 = A Panoramic View of Hainan Tourism and Culture：汉文、英文/吴文姝，杨蕾达著．—广州：暨南大学出版社，2019.8
ISBN 978 - 7 - 5668 - 2692 - 3

I.①海…　II.①吴…②杨…　III.①旅游文化—海南—汉、英　IV.①F592.766

中国版本图书馆 CIP 数据核字（2019）第 180139 号

海南旅游与文化概览
HAINAN LUYOU YU WENHUA GAILAN
著　者：吴文姝　杨蕾达

···

出 版 人：徐义雄
策划编辑：杜小陆
责任编辑：康　蕊
责任校对：王燕丽
责任印制：汤慧君　周一丹

出版发行：暨南大学出版社（510630）
电　　话：总编室（8620）85221601
　　　　　　营销部（8620）85225284　85228291　85228292（邮购）
传　　真：（8620）85221583（办公室）　85223774（营销部）
网　　址：http://www.jnupress.com
排　　版：广州良弓广告有限公司
印　　刷：广州市穗彩印务有限公司
开　　本：787mm×960mm　1/16
印　　张：12.75
字　　数：203 千
版　　次：2019 年 8 月第 1 版
印　　次：2019 年 8 月第 1 次
定　　价：56.00 元

Preface

In recent years, Hainan tourism industry has made many new achievements, and has become the most popular tropical island resort in China. It is now boosting ten tourism branches including marine tourism, recreational tourism, cultural and sports tourism, forest tourism, exhibition tourism, rural tourism, characteristic town tourism, shopping tourism, aerospace tourism and wedding tourism. The opening of more international direct flights has accelerated the integration of Hainan with the world, and promoted the international image of Hainan as "a sunshine Hainan, a holiday paradise".

Hainan tourism industry is developing very well, thanks to the central government's favorable policies. There are a lot of publicity materials on Hainan tourism in Chinese, but there is still a shortage of relevant English promotional materials. Therefore, in order to achieve sustainable development of Hainan tourism, it is imperative to introduce it to the world through multiple channels. On January 9th, 2019, the Hainan Provincial Government Office issued official document to promote citizens' foreign language proficiency in an all-round way, aiming at meeting the needs of building a Pilot Free Trade Zone (Port) with Chinese characteristics, cultivating citizens' awareness of openness and enhancing their foreign language cultural literacy and intercultural communicative competence. As we can see, English promotional materials on Hainan tourism and culture can be easier to be accepted by more foreigners, and make them desire to go to Hainan for leisure and vacation sightseeing.

The purpose of this book is to introduce Hainan's famous tourist attractions and local culture in English. It is hoped that Hainan can be more well-known. The first part of this book introduces the construction of Pilot Free Trade Zone (Port), tourism characteristics, humanistic history, all-round transport and the latest entry policy. In view of the distribution feature of Hainan's tourist resources, this book respectively introduces the tourist attractions and culture of Haikou, Sanya, Eastern Part, Western Part and Central Part of the island.

This book can be of great use to Hainan tourism industry, especially for English tour guides who can directly use it to introduce scenic spots and culture. It helps to enhance the soft power of Hainan tourism, as well. It is also a good book for college students and English learners to get to know Hainan tourism and culture.

In the process of compiling this book, we have consulted a lot of network materials, pictures, relevant books and documents. These references are listed at the end of the book to express our gratitude.

This book is planned and written by Wu Wenmei, School of Foreign Languages, Hainan Normal University. Yang Leida is in charge of proofreading. I would also like to express my sincere thanks to those teachers for their hard work in the process of completion of the book.

Wu Wenmei

January 26th, 2019

Contents

Part I Hainan Province

This part will focus on...

- construction of a Pilot Free Trade Zone;

- bays in Hainan;

- small islands in Hainan;

- Hainan tropical forests;

- Hainan historical and humanistic culture;

- Hainan cuisine;

- China Duty Free Mall;

- the all-directional travel transportation;

- the entry policy.

Chapter 1　Construction of a Pilot Free Trade Zone

Being the only tropical island-based province of China, Hainan features all-summer-like climate with average temperature of 23.8℃. Hainan is the second largest island of China, with a continent area of 35,000 square kilometers, covering over 2 million square kilometers of marine space. Haikou is the capital city of Hainan. Hainan has a population of 9.67 million based on the statistics of 2018.

In 1999, Hainan began to build itself into an ecological island, the first of its kind in China. In 2010, the State Council granted developing Hainan International Tourism Island. Endowed with superior natural environment and exclusive tourist resources, Hainan has enjoyed a high reputation by vacationers from home and abroad as an island of health, ecology and holidays. Up to 2017, a complete set of holiday and reception facilities have been in full service, and a team of well-trained service personnel have been in full readiness to guarantee a receiving capacity of over 60 million in a year.

Hainan has undergone great changes since it was approved to establish the special economic zone in 1988. Today Hainan is up for a new round of opening to the outside world at a wider scale, more extensive range and higher level. In April, 2018, President Xi Jinping announced that the Central Committee of the Communist Party of China had decided to support Hainan in developing the whole island into a Pilot Free Trade Zone, and gradually exploring and steadily promoting the establishment of a free trade port with Chinese characteristics. Hainan will be China's largest free trade zone enjoying higher-level opening-up policies. It will also be the country's first free trade port since the founding of People's Republic of China.

In developing the island into a Pilot Free Trade Zone, Hainan will be granted more autonomy to reform, and speed up the fostering of a law-based, international, and convenient business environment as well as a fair, open, unified, and efficient market environment. Focusing on sectors including medical care, education, sport, seeds, telecommunication and finance, the Pilot Free Trade Zone will push forward opening up of modern agriculture, high-tech industries and modern services, boost the development of service trade, protect the interests of overseas investors and promote the gradual opening-up of the shipping industry. In the development of the free trade port, Hainan should also enhance cooperation with countries and regions along the Belt and Road. Although Hainan used to be remote and underdeveloped, it has become one of China's most open and dynamic regions and also a window for the country's reform and opening-up.

Notes:

1. Endowed with superior natural environment and exclusive tourist resources, Hainan has enjoyed a high reputation by vacationers from home and abroad as an island

of health, ecology and holidays.

海南具有优越的自然环境和独特的旅游资源，以健康岛、生态岛和度假岛享誉海内外。

2. Hainan has undergone great changes since it was approved to establish the special economic zone in 1988.

海南自 1988 年被批准成立经济特区，已发生了巨大的变化。

3. In April, 2018, President Xi Jinping announced that the Central Committee of the Communist Party of China had decided to support Hainan in developing the whole island into a Pilot Free Trade Zone, and gradually exploring and steadily promoting the establishment of a free trade port with Chinese characteristics.

2018 年 4 月，习近平主席郑重宣布，中国共产党中央委员会已决定支持整个海南岛发展成一个自由贸易试验区，并逐步探索和稳步推进有中国特色的自由贸易港的建设。

4. In developing the island into a Pilot Free Trade Zone, Hainan will be granted more autonomy to reform, and speed up the fostering of a law-based, international, and convenient business environment as well as a fair, open, unified, and efficient market environment.

为建设自由贸易试验区，海南将被赋予更多的改革自主权，加快培育一个法制、国际、便利的商业环境，营造一个公平、开放、统一、高效的市场环境。

5. Although Hainan used to be remote and underdeveloped, it has become one of China's most open and dynamic regions and also a window for the country's reform and opening-up.

曾经偏远落后的海南，如今已成为中国最为开放的、最具活力的区域，同时也是中国改革开放的窗口。

Chapter 2   Bays in Hainan

Various bays in Hainan have attracted visitors from home and abroad. To see the sea in Hainan, in fact, is to see the bays. The famous bays include Yalong Bay, Haitang Bay, Dadonghai, Sanya Bay, Tianya Haijiao, Shimei Bay, Riyue Bay, Yueliang Bay, Holiday Beach, Qizi Bay and so on.

Bays in Sanya top the list in Hainan. Located at 18 degrees north latitude, Sanya is one of the most amazing geographical areas on the earth. This southernmost tourist city is blessed with the most pleasant climate, the freshest air, the warmest sunshine, the bluest sea water, the softest beach, etc. Therefore, beaches on these bays are better places to enjoy the attractions of the sea.

Yalong Bay boasts impressive beauty. The crescent-shaped bay is about 7. 5 kilometers long and covers an area of 18. 6 square kilometers. The scenery is gorgeous, with lush hills, amazingly blue sea and white sand beach. Tourists may also see well-preserved coral reefs and tropical fish of a great variety of types, colors and shapes. They can enjoy various entertainments and sports such as having fun on yachts, motorboats, or parasailing, and diving. They can also enjoy fresh sea food on the beach-front restaurants or in the restaurants in the hotels along the bay. The unique state-level tourist resort features seaside parks, deluxe villas, luxurious conference centers, five-star hotels, state-of-the-art golf courses and so on.

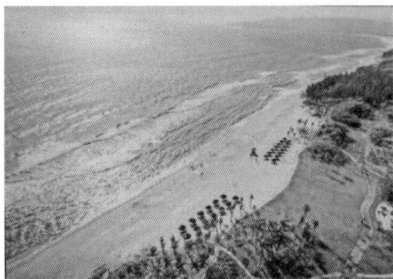

The coastline of Haitang Bay is 25 kilometers long. With fine beach and sand, it is very suitable for swimming. Compared to the other overdeveloped bays in Sanya, it is indeed quieter and purer. The beach here, far from the hustle and lust of the city, keeps a rare leisure and contentment. It is definitely worth visiting as there are Nantian Hot Springs, Iron Ore Harbor, Islamic tombs, Wuzhizhou Island, etc. Haitang Bay sits west to east, a good place to see the sunrise at sea.

Dadonghai has a crescent-shaped beach extending 2. 3 kilometers long. It is a wonderful place where clear blue sea, sunshine, and superb white sandy beach are so close to a city. Along the beach are well-designed sea-viewing wooden platforms with palm trees and pavilions. There are also many beach-front bars serving wine, beer, snacks and sea food along the area. The beach is ideal for recreational diving, beach volleyball, bathing and sunbathing. You can also enjoy driving motorboat, luxury yacht, having fun on a sail boat, experiencing ocean fishing, beach sports and underwater photography.

Sanya Bay is next to Sanya Phoenix International Airport, which stretches for 22 kilometers. Along the western part of Sanya Bay lies the 17. 8 kilometers Palm Tree Dream Avenue. On one side of the avenue is the area for star-rated hotels and modern beach-front residential blocks. On the other side of the avenue is the dream-like palm-fringed beach which is not as crowded as the beaches in Dadonghai or Yalong Bay. The most fascinating scene is the sunset on the Sanya Bay. Tourists will enjoy an amazing view of red and purple dusk sky, or a flaming sky that is overwhelmingly beautiful.

Tianya Haijiao is probably the most famous scenic spot on Hainan Island. Literally it means the end of sky and the rim of the sea in Chinese. Standing on the huge rocks on the beach, one can see the fantastic southern coastal scenery: the blue sea, the azure sky, the white waves and the yachts on the ocean in the distance. Scattering along the silvery beach are numerous rocks of various sizes and shapes. The most representative spot is a giant rock with Chinese characters meaning the end of sky and another one with Chinese characters meaning the rim of the sea.

Shimei Bay is a new and less visited beach along the east coast in Wanning. Its beach is ideal to anyone who is looking for a real quiet, isolated beach resort. Shimei Bay is also a nice choice for golf players with four clubs. If visitors just want to lie on the beach, enjoy the crystal-clear water, sandy beach and resorts facilities, Shimei Bay is the perfect place to go. Besides beach and pool, there are some recreations available: water sports, Spa, cycling, wind surfing, reading... or just lying on the beach with a favorite novel. Or they could visit local areas by bike or take a tour to the biggest Botanical Garden, or enjoy hot spring in Xinglong.

In short, these bays are ideal leisure destinations destined to become international seashore resorts emphasizing ecological tourism and dedicated to quality service. They are excellent choices for your holiday.

Notes:

1. This southernmost tourist city is blessed with the most pleasant climate, the freshest air, the warmest sunshine, the bluest sea water, the softest beach, etc.

这个最南端的旅游城市拥有最宜人的气候，最新鲜的空气，最温暖的阳光，最湛蓝的海水，最柔软的海滩等。

2. The unique state-level tourist resort features seaside parks, deluxe villas, luxurious conference centers, five-star hotels, state-of-the-art golf courses and so on.

这个独特的国家级旅游度假区有海滨公园、豪华别墅、豪华会议中心、五星级酒店、最先进的高尔夫球场等。

3. It is definitely worth visiting as there are Nantian Hot Springs, Iron Ore Harbor, Islamic tombs, Wuzhizhou Island, etc.

它绝对值得参观，因为那儿有南天温泉、铁矿石港、伊斯兰教墓、蜈支洲岛等。

4. Tourists will enjoy an amazing view of red and purple dusk sky, or a flaming sky that is overwhelmingly beautiful.

游客会欣赏到惊艳的景象，天空时红时紫，或出现绚丽多彩的火烧云。

5. If visitors just want to lie on the beach, enjoy the crystal-clear water, sandy beach and resorts facilities, Shimei Bay is the perfect place to go.

如果游客只是想躺在沙滩上，享受清澈的水、沙滩和度假村，石梅湾是最好的地方。

6. In short, these bays are ideal leisure destinations destined to become international seashore resorts emphasizing ecological tourism and dedicated to quality service.

总之，这些海湾个个都是理想的休闲胜地，致力于发展成绿色生态、优质服务的国际海滨度假胜地。

Chapter 3   Small Islands in Hainan

Various bays apart, small islands with beautiful scenery abound, such as Wuzhizhou Island, West Island, the Boundary Island, Nanwan Monkey Island, Dazhou Island as well.

Wuzhizhou Island is about 1.48 square kilometers with a coastal line of 5.7 kilometers. Tropical plants flourish on this green island. The brilliantly colorful coral reefs make it the best place for scuba diving in China. In the typically crystal clear sea water, tourists can experience the unique and beautiful underwater scenery which is a treasure house of a great variety of fish, corals, and other marine denizens. In addition, surfing is also a sensational bonus to holiday experience for water sport enthusiasts.

West Island is often called as an island for sports. On this island, tourists can enjoy a great variety of entertainments and sports such as having fun on yachts, motorboats, sailboats, banana boats, or parasailing, water skiing, glass-bottom boat sightseeing, sea angling, and diving. They can also enjoy fresh sea food on the beach-front restaurants near the sea angling platform. They may also have a chance to see natural coral reefs, various species of salt water fish, sting rays, and turtles!

The Boundary Island is a pretty small island which is located in the South Sea off Lingshui. The eastern part of the island features sheer cliffs and white waves and foams dashing over the rocks on the shoreline. On the west side, there is a small beach with clean white sand and palm trees. There are also some facilities for recreation, such as yachts, motorboats, sailboats, banana boats, or parasailing. Visitors may also see everything from tropical sea-water fish to various corals and rock formations on the island.

Nanwan Monkey Island is filled with fun and excitement. Visitors can ride the longest oversea rope-way in Hainan to have a wonderful view of the ocean, the fishing rafts by the bank and the thick chains of mountains on the island. The most exciting thing on the island is to watch all kinds of macaques. Upon walking through a vegetation corridor, visitors are amazed to find seven or eight macaques standing in a line along the path with triangular flags and saluting to welcome their honored guests. In the pond, some of them dive, some swim freestyle, and some even do the breaststroke. They are so amused that visitors can't help applauding and clapping for them. What's more, their circus performances are terrific and are allowed to take photos.

To the southeast of Wanning is Dazhou Island, 15 kilometers away from Wanning. Dazhou Island covers an area of 4.36 square kilometers and it is made up of two smaller islands and three peaks. Dazhou Island is China's only production base for bird's nest, a Chinese delicacy known for its health benefits. Many varieties of flora and fauna reside on

Dazhou Island. With its amazingly clear waters and beautiful mountain scenery, Dazhou Island is a wonderful place to visit. The sea around the island is a famous large fishing ground for the fishermen from Sanya, Lingshui and other places. Among them, the number of private boats is numerous. Their whole family lives on the boat, and they fish all the year round, calling the island the second home of their family.

These small islands are rather distinctive, waiting for you to explore.

Notes:

1. The brilliantly colorful coral reefs make it the best place for scuba diving in China.

绚丽多彩的珊瑚礁使它成为中国潜水最好的地方。

2. The eastern part of the island features sheer cliffs and white waves and foams dashing over the rocks on the shoreline.

岛的东部以陡峭的悬崖著称，白浪冲刷海岸线上的岩石，泡沫飞溅。

3. Visitors can ride the longest oversea rope-way in Hainan to have a wonderful view of the ocean, the fishing rafts by the bank and the thick chains of mountains on the island.

游客可乘坐海南最长的海上索道欣赏大海的美景、岸边的渔筏、岛上连绵不断的山脉。

4. In the pond, some of them dive, some swim freestyle, and some even do the breaststroke.

在池里，有的（猕猴）潜水，有的游自由泳，有的甚至游蛙泳。

5. Dazhou Island is China's only production base for bird's nest, a Chinese delicacy known for its health benefits.

大洲岛是中国唯一的燕窝生产基地，它是一道闻名遐迩的、健康的中国佳肴。

Chapter 4　Hainan Tropical Forests

Hainan Island is said to be one of the purest islands that remains unpolluted. Over 62.1% of the island area is covered by forest, ranking No. 4 nationwide by the end of year 2017. All kinds of eco-tourist products, tropical rainforest ventures and forest recreational services are popular among visitors from home and abroad. The fresh air and the greenness that spreads in all directions are the natural gifts Hainan has to offer.

There are five major tropical primitive forests in Hainan distributed over the Wuzhi Mountain, Limu Mountain, Diaoluo Mountain, Jianfengling, Bawangling in its interior and they contain numerous different species of wildlife.

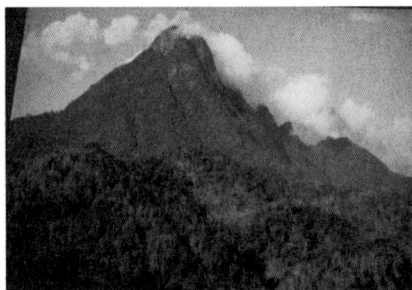

Crowned as "the Roof of Hainan", Wuzhi Mountain is located at the center of Hainan Island. Its main peak rises as high as 1,867 meters, the highest in the province. Wuzhi Mountain nature reserve is the largest of its kind in Hainan. It is also a nature reserve with the most typical tropical rainforest, the highest altitude, the biggest relative elevation, the richest tropical vegetation form and the most complete vegetation vertical zonation. A visit to this area will reward you with the scenic wonder of the main peak and impressive waterfalls. Adventurers can take an opportunity to float down the mountain streams and experience the excitement of Hainan summer. Visitors can experience the special customs and culture of the minority of Li and Miao as well.

Limu Mountain Forest Park lies in Qiongzhong Li and Miao Autonomous County, the central part of Hainan Province. With the highest altitude of 1,411 meters, it covers an area of 12,900 hectares, among which natural forest accounts for 7,300 hectares. As a tropical rainforest, it is rich in tropical biological resources including more than 2,000 kinds of plants and 58 kinds of rare or endangered wild animals. As one of the three great mountains in Hainan, Limu Mountain features numerous waterfalls. It is one of the most diversified scenic parks in all of Hainan, featuring rugged mountains and vast woodlands. Limu Mountain is a sacred place for the Li nationality, the earliest inhabitants of Hainan Province, who still remain a simple lifestyle with unique traditional customs. With a number of great trails for hikes, Limu Mountain is one of the most fulfilling locations in Hainan.

Diaoluo Mountain is a paradise for plants because of an average temperature of 20℃ and an annual rainfall of 2,160 millimeters. It is a natural Botanic Garden as well. There are 3,500 different kinds of plants and 250 species of flowers in the forest. The forest is also a treasure place of Chinese herbal medicines. The mountain is abundant with 112 species of birds and 34 species of animals. Diaoluo Mountain mainly differs from other mountains in its water, featuring with waterfalls, streams and ponds everywhere! The most famous one is the 100-meter-high Fengguoshan Waterfall cluster. For those living in urban areas, wandering along the lakes and falls can give them a feeling of returning back to nature.

Jianfengling is known as "China's top ten most beautiful forest". Tropical rainforest and rare animals such as gibbon, peacock pheasant are put under protection. 85% of wildlife plants in Hainan are growing in this mysterious big forest. Jianfengling region has preserved the whole area of China's largest tropical forest. The integrity of the vegetation and species of diversity ranks the first, followed by the Amazon, the

Congo River and Southeast Asian tropical rainforest. This Park Forest is covered by ancient towering trees, vines, streams, flowing cloud together. It is silent among the mountain, especially by Tianchi pond at an altitude of 600 meters. In summer, cool wind blows gently, and the air is fresh, so it is a good summer resort.

Bawangling covers an area of 67 square kilometers, being known as one of the richest resources of the country. UNESCO has also established a research base for biological science here. Thanks to the unique natural conditions and best-preserved ecosystem, rare species of animals and plants flourish, including the endangered species—the Hainan gibbon. In the reserve, there are more than 600 tree species, among which 27 species are well protected. Bawangling Nature Reserve is one of the best remaining tropical forests in China, and has recently been identified as an important bird base in the Indo-Burmese Forests.

Apart from the above five major tropical primitive forests, Hainan Yanoda Rainforest Cultural Tourism Zone is a perfect place for the unique rainforest at 18 degrees north latitude. The Rainforest Valley contains six rainforest wonders such as plant strangle, flower basket, old stems blossom, great roots, intertwined vines and huge stones embraced by roots. All these natural scenes are symbolizing the essential features of the five major rainforests in Hainan Island. In the valleys, the plank roads are carefully designed according to the landscape and the mountain terrain and lead to the deep forest.

Stepping on the stone stairs twisted up at both sides of the huge rocks, visitors can feel the tranquility and the mystery in the deep forest. They can also enjoy the joyfulness of playing waterfalls, and experience the pleasant surprise and the quiver of emotion on the fantastic suspension bridges in Yanoda.

For the people who prefer the green mountains and forests, the tropical primeval rainforest will fit their travel need.

Notes:

1. A visit to this area will reward you with the scenic wonder of the main peak and impressive waterfalls.

到这个地方旅游将让您有机会领略主峰的奇观风景和引人注目的瀑布。

2. Limu Mountain is a sacred place for the Li nationality, the earliest inhabitants of Hainan Province, who still remain a simple lifestyle with unique traditional customs.

黎母山是海南省最早居民——黎族人的圣地，他们仍保留简单的、独特的传统风俗和生活方式。

3. Diaoluo Mountain mainly differs from other mountains in its water, featuring with waterfalls, streams and ponds everywhere!

吊罗山和其他山之间的主要区别是水多，到处都有瀑布、溪流和池塘。

4. The integrity of the vegetation and species of diversity ranks the first, followed by the Amazon, the Congo River and Southeast Asian tropical rainforest.

整个地区的植被的完整性和物种的多样性都名列前茅，其次是亚马逊河、刚果河和东南亚的热带雨林。

5. The Rainforest Valley contains six rainforest wonders such as plant strangle, flower basket, old stems blossom, great roots, intertwined vines and huge stones embraced by roots.

雨林谷有六种雨林奇观，如植物绞杀、空中花篮、老茎生花、藤本攀附、高板根、根包石。

Chapter 5   Hainan Historical and Humanistic Culture

Hainan history can be dated back to Han Dynasty when the Han government established two prefectures, Zhuya and Dan' er on the island. With such a long history, Hainan Island has rich historical and cultural resources. Walking through the old buildings, and looking for the most ancient atmosphere, we seem to travel back to thousands of years ago, and appreciate the wisdom of our ancestors.

To explore Hainan history, the Five-Lord Temple is a popular destination for tourists which commemorates five disgraced high-ranking central government officials during the Tang and Song Dynasties. They were Li Deyu, Li Gang, Zhao Ding, Li Guang and Hu Quan. The main hall of No. 1 Building in Hainan houses the lifelike stone statues of the five prestigious officials. Sugong Temple, located in the east of the Five-Lord Temple, is another fascinating destination. Having been renovated over dynasties, this historical site has helped understand Hainan history, political and cultural development.

It is well known that this island was traditionally a place of exile for disgraced officials, but on the other hand, their arrival have brought well-being to the local people. The exiled official and poet Su Shi (Su Dongpo) came to Danzhou and made a great contribution to spreading education in the local place. To commemorate him, Dongpo Academy of Classical Learning was first built in 1098, and now it has become a tourist attraction. Its main attraction—Zai Jiu Tang in Chinese, is a second-row courtyard where Su Dongpo gave lectures and chatted with his friends. In the lobby, east and west wings are displayed piles of Su' s works of calligraphy, paintings, and historic manuscripts.

Walking along Deshengsha Street, Bo' ai Street or Zhongshan Street in Haikou, you'll find exotic landscapes of Qilou Arcades. Based on historical record, the first Qilou building in Haikou was built in 1894 at Sipailou Street, which is now called North Bo' ai Street. Historically, the street had housed consulates, churches, post offices, banks and chambers of commerce belonging to 13 different countries. Viewed from the distance, buildings with three or four stores in height are linked together. Technically, its ground floor set back halfway into the building to take shelter from rain and sunlight so that it can be used as a storefront. The upper floors serve as the living quarters, and extend over the pavement supported by columns. Today, it remains Haikou's business center with a taste of traditional life of Haikou. Undoubtedly, Qilou Arcade Street is a lively history book of Haikou, and it was selected as one of the 10 Historical and Cultural Streets of China in 2007.

Salt has always been an essential ingredient for human beings. Back to 1,200 years ago, a group of migrant workers in Danzhou discovered new methods of making salt. They made a groundbreaking achievement by drilling rocks to make containers for sea water, exposing them in the sun and extracting salt from sea water. Because this way created a precedent for the high yield of "sun salt", Emperor Qianlong of the Qing Dynasty gave credit to these workers. Later these fields are referred as "Millennium Ancient Salt Fields", which are now located in Yangpu Peninsula.

No place like a museum can make you fully explore the history of a place. Hainan Provincial Museum is the only comprehensive modern museum of Hainan Province. The museum has four basic exhibition series: "Exhibition of Collected Cultural Relics" " Exhibition of History of Hainan " "Exhibition of Marine Civilization in the South China Sea" and "Exhibition of Intangible Cultural Heritage in Hainan". One can get acquainted with a comprehensive history of Hainan, culture of national minorities, intangible cultural heritage and cultural relics. Currently, the museum possesses more than 20,000 collection items. In the museum, visitors can have access to the rich cultural relics via vivid settings and multimedia. In this way, they can understand and experience the unique historical inheritance and cultural atmosphere of Hainan in a multi-layer manner.

Hainan is a multicultural society with various minorities, so it boasts both unique minority cultures and diversified festive galas, among which the most influential ones are: Fucheng Flower Exchanging Festival in February, Haikou Madam

Xian Cultural Festival in March, Lunar March 3rd Li and Miao Cultural Festival, Dragon Water Festival in June, Danzhou Singing Festival in September, Nanshan Longevity Cultural Festival in October, Hainan Island Carnival, Sanya International Wedding Festival in December. Whenever you come to Hainan, you will enjoy a tour to its fullest.

If you happen to spend holiday in Sanya and feel fascinated by this charming city, you may as well visit Sanya Romance Park for "The Legend of Romance" performance. It tells the history of Sanya from ancient time to modern ones through acrobatics, dance, and music. The one-hour shows featuring Sanya culture are performed at the theater daily, which can seat 4,700 people. The show has become the reputed program of the theme park and representative show in Sanya.

The best way to feel about culture is to experience it, to listen, to see, to touch, and to feel it. So welcome to experience the charm of Hainan in person.

Notes:

1. The main hall of No. 1 Building in Hainan houses the lifelike stone statues of the five prestigious officials.

海南第一楼大殿里摆着栩栩如生的五公石像。

2. It is well known that this island was traditionally a place of exile for disgraced officials, but on the other hand, their arrival have brought well-being to the local people.

众所周知，这个岛以前是流放被贬官员的地方，不过他们的到来也给当地人民带来了福祉。

3. Historically, the street had housed consulates, churches, post offices, banks

and chambers of commerce belonging to 13 different countries.

历史上，这条街曾经驻有 13 个国家的领事馆、教堂、邮局、银行和商会。

4. Because this way created a precedent for the high yield of "sun salt", Emperor Qianlong of the Qing Dynasty gave credit to these workers.

因为这种方式开创了"日晒盐"高产的先例，盐田人受到清朝皇帝乾隆的嘉奖。

5. The museum has four basic exhibition series："Exhibition of Collected Cultural Relics" "Exhibition of History of Hainan" "Exhibition of Marine Civilization in the South China Sea" and "Exhibition of Intangible Cultural Heritage in Hainan".

博物馆共有四个系列的基础陈列："海南风情陈列""海南历史陈列""南海海洋文明陈列"和"海南少数民族非遗陈列"。

Chapter 6   Hainan Cuisine

Hainan Cuisine has several big characteristics: fresh, light, natural, and unique. It has derived from Guangdong cuisine and shared much in common with it. Morning tea in Guangdong style has been popular in most of restaurants, so much so that it develops to afternoon tea and evening tea. It features natural flavor of food, without adding too many sauces. Water-oiled meat, vegetables and sea food are favored by most local people, which also account for the secret of local people's longevity. Hainan cuisine also includes local food of ethnic minorities such as Li and Miao.

The four famous Hainan dishes truly live up to their fame, namely Wenchang chicken, Jiaji duck, Hele crab and Dongshan mutton. Among them, Wenchang chicken may be the most well-known. Not only popular in Hainan, it has become a signature dish in Hong Kong and Southeast Asia. The traditional way of cooking

Wenchang chicken is to boil it in water within a strictly controlled period of time, then cut it into pieces, and eat it with mixture of vinegar, chopped ginger and sesame oil. The cooking way of Jiaji duck is quite similar to that of Wenchang chicken. Wanning, where the three local rivers meet, provides a perfect home for Hele crab. The best time for eating Hele crab is late summer and early fall. It is often served with a dipping sauce made from ginger, garlic and vinegar. Dongshan mutton is famous for its aromatic and non-greasy meat. It is often cooked with special seasoning and ingredients. With red color and savory taste, it is truly appealing and perfect to eat when served in hot pot.

Hainan Island is a paradise for seafood, and the seafood square is the best choice. There are all kinds of fresh and vigorous seafood and vegetables, whose prices are similar to those in the farmers' markets. Visitors can first go to the market to select seafood and vegetables and fruits according to their personal preferences, and then choose the stalls for processing and cooking. The prices of seafood are fair, and the variety of seafood is abundant, which is the most attractive charm. An array of delicacies surely delight the guests' eye, such as garlic oysters, boiled prawns, mantis shrimps fried with salt and pepper, steamed crabs, etc. Every evening, a substantial number of diners from all over the country come to eat in the seafood courts.

In Hainan, there is another way of cooking seafood—put it in an earthen kiln and roast it on fire. The procedure is to season fresh seafood first and wrap it in tin paper. At the same time, the earth stoves are being heated and then the seafood wrapped is put in a big iron bucket to roast. After about half an hour, the seafood can be served. As soon as the tin paper is opened, the fragrance of seafood rushes out. This cooking method ensures the nutrition of the food and the delicious taste.

Wenchang chicken coconut soup is one of the most representative dishes in Hainan cuisine. It is famous for its delicious soup and tender chicken. It is popular in Hainan Island. With fresh coconut juice as soup, Wenchang chicken is stewed slowly over a small fire. The soup contains both the sweetness of coconut juice and the fragrance of chicken. It is nourishing and delicious. It is really a gourmet feast that can not be missed. Coconut chicken is served in the hotpot. After the soup is boiled, the chicken can be poured in and boiled. Because the meat is fresh and tender, it only takes five minutes to cook the meat thoroughly. The chicken has little fat and there is no greasy chicken oil in the soup. When it is ready, you might as well have a bowl of chicken soup before eating meat. At this time, the soup is the sweetest and best. Chicken tastes delicate and tender, together with spicy and sour sauce. You can always make your own special sauce by adding chopped garlic, green kumquat, ginger, pepper, assorted sauce, soy sauce, vinegar and so on.

While travelling around the island, tourists can also take time to savor Hainan famous snacks. Hainan rice noodles are both snack and staple food for the locals. They eat them for breakfast and during festivals, and serve them to guests. Originally, this dish was created in Haikou, and was loved by urban residents of the city, so it was soon spread to the rest of the island. Traditionally, the noodles are usually topped with meat sauce, roasted peanuts and slices of bamboo. Famous rice noodles also include Baoluo rice noodles and Lingshui sour rice noodles. Their ingredients and making are slightly different and cater to different people.

Assorted beans and corns in icy coconut juice (*Qingbuliang* in Chinese) is a cool refreshing dessert. It is known for the healthy ingredients and regarded as the best dessert in Hainan, so much so that it is popular all the year round, especially in hot summer days. Common ingredients include dates, mung beans, barley, taros, watermelons, quail eggs, nuts, and more, but you can choose whichever you want in icy coconut milk or syrup. It is delicious as well as nutritious.

Fried ice is icy and tasteful and the flavor is up to you! Pick your favorite combination of fresh fruits, which will be blended with condensed milk and then stir-fried until it is frozen into a kind of fresh fruit sorbet. Kiwi, banana, or mango are very popular. Toppings includes chopped nuts and raisins which are optional.

Rice noodle rolls is a very popular Hainan breakfast dish. Filled with bits of meat or vegetables, the rolls are then eaten with soy sauce or hot sauce. These breakfast noodles are often sold at street stalls and carts, or at local breakfast spots. The rice noodle wrapper is thin and tender, and the fillings are savory.

Zongzi is made of glutinous rice stuffed with different fillings and wrapped in bamboo, reed, or other large flat leaves. It is cooked by steaming or boiling. It is traditionally eaten during the Dragon Boat Festival which falls on the fifth day of the fifth month of the lunar calendar. Hainan Zongzi is larger than other types, with large amounts of fillings. In Hainan, Zongzi fillings can include pork, chicken, salted duck eggs, shrimp, shredded squid, and more. Danzhou Zongzi and Ding' an Zongzi have enjoyed high reputation in Hainan Island and they are often sent as gifts to friends or relatives in the season of Dragon Boat Festival.

All in all, Hainan cuisine is light and fresh, with plenty of seafood, fruit, and snacks! The freshness and quality of the ingredients are showcased for the tourists.

Notes：

1. Morning tea in Guangdong style has been popular in most of restaurants，so much so that it develops to afternoon tea and evening tea.

粤式早茶在很多餐馆都受欢迎，以至于下午茶和晚茶也盛行。

2. In Hainan，there is another way of cooking seafood—put it in an earthen kiln and roast it on fire.

在海南，海鲜还有另外一种吃法——放进土窑里用火烧。

3. Wenchang chicken coconut soup is one of the most representative dishes in Hainan cuisine. It is famous for its delicious soup and tender chicken.

在海南美食中，文昌椰子鸡汤是最具有代表性的本帮菜之一，以汤汁鲜香、鸡肉滑嫩而著称。

4. It is traditionally eaten during the Dragon Boat Festival which falls on the fifth day of the fifth month of the lunar calendar.

传统上都是在农历五月初五端午节吃粽子。

5. The freshness and quality of the ingredients are showcased for the tourists.

（海南菜）向游客展示了原料的新鲜和品质。

Chapter 7   China Duty Free Mall

One of the biggest attractions in Sanya is the duty-free shopping mall where you can buy international brands without going to an international airport. The fascinating China Duty Free (CDF) Mall is the world's largest duty free shopping centre, built at a cost of over five billion yuan, and is located in the Haitang Bay area.

Covering an area of 70,000 square meters, the CDF Mall integrates duty-free shopping, duty-paid shopping, restaurants, entertainment venues and cultural facilities. Top of the line international brands have big outlets at the mall. The duty-free shopping done at the mall can be collected at the mall's counters inside Sanya airport's check-in.

The unique aesthetic design of the mall is inspired by the Haitang flower, the symbol of Sanya. Its atrium is formed by four unique curved surfaced steel structures, which enable natural light to filter into the mall and create a world-class shopping environment for the users. Its unique 3D free surfaced steel structure covers entrance arch-truss, link-bridges and other five individual skylights.

The mall opened in September 2014 and shuttle buses are available to ferry visitors and shoppers from hotels and resorts and even residential areas.

Notes:

1. The fascinating China Duty Free (CDF) Mall is the world's largest duty free shopping centre, built at a cost of over five billion yuan, and is located in the Haitang Bay area.

位于海棠湾的迷人的中国免税（CDF）购物中心是世界上最大的免税购物中心，建设成本超过五十亿元。

2. Covering an area of 70,000 square meters, the CDF Mall integrates duty-free shopping, duty-paid shopping, restaurants, entertainment venues and cultural facilities.

中国免税购物中心面积达 70 000 平方米，共三层，包括免税购物、完税购物、餐饮、娱乐场所和文化设施。

3. The unique aesthetic design of the mall is inspired by the Haitang flower, the symbol of Sanya.

购物中心独特的美学设计灵感来自三亚的象征——海棠花。

4. Its atrium is formed by four unique curved surfaced steel structures, which enable natural light to filter into the mall and create a world-class shopping environment for the users.

它的中庭是由四个独特的曲面钢结构构成，自然光能透入商场，为顾客创造一个世界级购物环境。

5. The mall opened in September 2014 and shuttle buses are available to ferry visitors and shoppers from hotels and resorts and even residential areas.

购物中心于 2014 年 9 月开张，穿梭巴士为来自酒店、度假胜地甚至居民区的游客和购物者提供接送服务。

Chapter 8   The All-directional Travel Transportation

Transportation in Hainan has been developing at a fast pace and has established a relatively complete operating network, including air, high-speed railway, expressway and sea transport.

Air

There are two international airports in Hainan: Haikou Meilan International Airport in the North and Sanya Phoenix International Airport in the South. They both have flights among 37 cities home and abroad.   Qionghai Bo' ao Airport is a newly-opened airport in March, 2016. Up to February 8th, 2017, 26 domestic routes have been opened.   In addition, there are some special mini-airports throughout the province, so it will be quite convenient to catch a flight from wherever you are in Hainan.

High-Speed Railway

海南省环岛铁路平面示意图

The Eastern Ring High-Speed Railway runs along Hainan's east coast between Haikou and Sanya, stopping at many coastal cities along the way, including Wenchang, Qionghai, Wanning, and more. The trains are designed to travel at approximately 250 km/h and currently stop at 15 stations along the line. The total length of the route is 308.11 kilometers and its total travel time is 1 hour and 26 minutes.

The much-anticipated Hainan Western Ring High-Speed Railway officially opened on December 20th, 2015. The train travels at a speed of 200 km/h, and it takes 1 hour and 56 minutes for the train to cover the 345-kilometer distance.

All ticket prices and timetables can be checked on China's official Railway website: www. 12306. cn. This modern high-speed train provides a comfortable, convenient, and affordable way to travel around the island.

Expressway

As one of the main means of land transportation in Hainan, expressways spread throughout the province. The total length of expressways in Hainan is more than 17,000 kilometers. There are trunk roads connecting ports, cities and counties across the island, as well as branch roads to villages, towns and all tourist sites. The round-the-island expressway enables a short drive of just three hours from Haikou in the North to Sanya in the South.

Tourists now are able to take a coach from many cities in mainland China to Hainan Province as well, such as Guangzhou, Zhuhai, Zhanjiang, Nanning, Chongqing, etc.

The Luxurious Cruiser

Hainan is an ocean-based province in the embrace of boundless waters, featuring the same latitude and climate conditions as Florida, America. Haikou and Sanya in general are one of the top 5 cruiser economic regions of China. Currently, the Sanya-based 100,000-ton-capacity

cruiser wharf has come into operation. Cruisers have become another popular tool of access to Sanya. Therefore, you can choose Sanya and Haikou as your cruiser holiday destinations, enjoying your sea-based holidays and passion and romance of Hainan with your business partners, friends or families.

Notes:

1. Transportation in Hainan has been developing at a fast pace and has established a relatively complete operating network, including air, high-speed railway, expressway and sea transport.

海南交通发展迅速，建立了较为完整的运营网络，包括空运、高速铁路、高速公路和海上运输。

2. In addition, there are some special mini-airports throughout the province, so it will be quite convenient to catch a flight from wherever you are in Hainan.

此外，全省各地还有一些特殊的小型机场，所以无论您在海南哪个地方，搭乘航班都非常方便。

3. The Eastern Ring High-Speed Railway runs along Hainan's east coast between Haikou and Sanya, stopping at many coastal cities along the way, including Wenchang, Qionghai, Wanning, and more.

东环高铁沿海南东海岸途经海口和三亚，沿途停靠点包括文昌、琼海、万宁等多个沿海城市。

4. This modern high-speed train provides a comfortable, convenient, and affordable way to travel around the island.

这种现代化的高铁提供舒适、方便、经济实惠的环岛旅行。

5. As one of the main means of land transportation in Hainan, expressways spread throughout the province.

高速公路作为海南的主要交通工具之一，在省内四通八达。

Chapter 9   The Entry Policy

On April 18th, 2018, the Ministry of Public Security of the People's Republic of China and the State Immigration Administration held a news conference to announce the important news that, starting from May 1st, 2018, citizens of 59 countries may enjoy 30-day visa-free access to Hainan Island. The new policy is an attempt to support island's reform and opening-up.

The 59 counties that may enjoy visa-free access to Hainan include: Russia, the United Kingdom, France, Germany, Norway, Ukraine, Italy, Austria, Finland, the Netherlands, Denmark, Switzerland, Sweden, Spain, Belgium, Czech Republic, Estonia, Greece, Hungary, Iceland, Latvia, Lithuania, Luxemburg, Malta, Poland, Portugal, Slovakia, Slovenia, Ireland, Cyprus, Bulgaria, Romania, Serbia, Croatia,

Bosnia and Herzegovina, Montenegro, Macedonia, Albania, the United States, Canada, Brazil, Mexico, Argentina, Chile, Australia, New Zealand, South Korea, Japan, Singapore, Malaysia, Thailand, Kazakhstan, the Philippines, Indonesia, Brunei, Monaco, Belarus, UAE and Qatar.

According to the State Immigration Administration, the visa-free policy for the entry of the 59-nation personnel will include the following three main aspects. The first is to expand the scope of visa-free countries. Countries that have applied for a visa-free entry policy have been liberalized from 26 countries to 59 countries, which is conducive to encouraging more foreigners to travel to Hainan to form a more open new pattern. The second is to extend the visa-free stay. After the visa-free entry, the stay time was uniformly extended from 15 or 21 days to 30 days, which promoted more active development of the inbound tourism market. The third is to relax restrictions on the number of exemptions. Under the premise of retaining the invitation mode of the travel agency invitation, the team will be exempted from visa waiver as a personal visa exemption to meet the individual travel needs of foreign tourists. This visa-free policy can be simply referred to as "enlargement, extension, and relaxation".

According to the regulations, if you need to go to other provinces after entering Hainan for legitimate reasons, or if you need to stay in Hainan for more than the time limit for visa exemption, you may apply to the Exit and Entry Administration Department of the local Public Security Bureau to apply for a stay permit. It will provide convenience according to law.

Notes:

The 59 counties that may enjoy visa-free access to Hainan include: Russia, the United Kingdom, France, Germany, Norway, Ukraine, Italy, Austria, Finland, the Netherlands, Denmark, Switzerland, Sweden, Spain, Belgium, Czech Republic, Estonia, Greece, Hungary, Iceland, Latvia, Lithuania, Luxemburg, Malta, Poland, Portugal, Slovakia, Slovenia, Ireland, Cyprus, Bulgaria, Romania, Serbia, Croatia,

Bosnia and Herzegovina, Montenegro, Macedonia, Albania, the United States, Canada, Brazil, Mexico, Argentina, Chile, Australia, New Zealand, South Korea, Japan, Singapore, Malaysia, Thailand, Kazakhstan, the Philippines, Indonesia, Brunei, Monaco, Belarus, UAE and Qatar.

　　59 国人员入境海南旅游免签证，包括：俄罗斯、英国、法国、德国、挪威、乌克兰、意大利、奥地利、芬兰、荷兰、丹麦、瑞士、瑞典、西班牙、比利时、捷克、爱沙尼亚、希腊、匈牙利、冰岛、拉脱维亚、立陶宛、卢森堡、马耳他、波兰、葡萄牙、斯洛伐克、斯洛文尼亚、爱尔兰、塞浦路斯、保加利亚、罗马尼亚、塞尔维亚、克罗地亚、波黑、黑山、马其顿、阿尔巴尼亚、美国、加拿大、巴西、墨西哥、阿根廷、智利、澳大利亚、新西兰、韩国、日本、新加坡、马来西亚、泰国、哈萨克斯坦、菲律宾、印度尼西亚、文莱、摩纳哥、白俄罗斯、阿联酋、卡塔尔。

Part Ⅱ Haikou

This part will focus on...

- general introduction to Haikou;
- Five-Lord Temple;
- Shishan Volcanic Cluster National Geopark;
- Dongzhai Harbor Mangrove Natural Reserve Area;
- Holiday Beach Resort;
- Qilou Arcades;
- Hairui Tomb;
- Feng Xiaogang Movie Town.

Chapter 1　General Introduction to Haikou

Haikou, also known as the "Coconut City", is the capital of Hainan Province. The city is the provincial administrative center of Hainan, being the focus of the local economy, culture and transportation in the meanwhile. Haikou stands at the northern end of Hainan Island, on the west bank of the Nandu River estuary. This river is the longest on the island and the city's name appropriately means "Mouth of the Sea".

With the sea on three sides, Haikou enjoys a long coastline that features excellent bathing beaches and seaside resorts. Holiday Beach is the most popular of these, while Xixiu Beach is the spot where the national sailing and windsurfing teams train and hold competitions.

The downtown area of the city has an excellent environment with streets lined with coconut palms. Here and there are modern and convenient public transport facilities, which meet the needs of the tourist in a friendly and welcoming way. Hainan Meilan International Airport, railway station, ship and expressway link cities of China and the whole world.

Besides its natural resources, there are several important sites of historical interest in Haikou. Five-Lord Temple, Hai Rui Tomb and the Xiuying Battery serve as reminders of the historical importance of Haikou.

No trip is complete without the opportunity to savor tempting local food and shopping opportunities. It goes without saying that for anyone coming to Haikou, seafood is definitely a must. However, the city is also famous for its other prized dishes. There are four famous dishes to delight the gourmet and should not be missed. Moreover, they are other well-known local dishes and snacks, such as Stewed Beef Brisket with Rice, Pig Feet in Brown Sauce with Rice, morning tea in Cantonese Style, Hainan Noodles, Assorted Beans and Corns in Icy Coconut Juice and so on. There is an abundance of fresh local fruits such as mangos, pineapples, jackfruits, coconuts, carambola, papaya, longan and lichee, loquat, naseberry and passion fruit. Maybe some of these will be new to you but if you try them you will want to take more home!

Haikou has evolved from a simple sightseeing city to an attractive seaside resort and business center. The services for visitors to the city are being extended with the aim of establishing Haikou as Southern China's key center for tourism.

Notes:

1. The city is the provincial administrative center of Hainan, being the focus of

the local economy, culture and transportation in the meanwhile.

海口市是海南省的省级行政中心，同时也是当地经济、文化、交通的中心。

2. The downtown area of the city has an excellent environment with streets lined with coconut palms.

市中心环境优美，街道两旁种着椰子树。

3. Besides its natural resources, there are several important sites of historical interest in Haikou.

除了自然资源以外，海口还有几处重要的名胜古迹。

4. No trip is complete without the opportunity to savor tempting local food and shopping opportunities.

只有品尝了当地美食和体验购物，旅途才算是完美。

5. Haikou has evolved from a simple sightseeing city to an attractive seaside resort and business center.

海口已经从一个简单的观光城市发展成为一个吸引人的海滨度假胜地和商务中心。

Chapter 2 Five-Lord Temple

The Five-Lord Temple, located in Haifu Road, was originally constructed during the reign of Emperor Wanli in the Ming Dynasty. It was renovated on several occasions during the Qing Dynasty. Now, it is a place known for honoring the great figures in the history of Hainan.

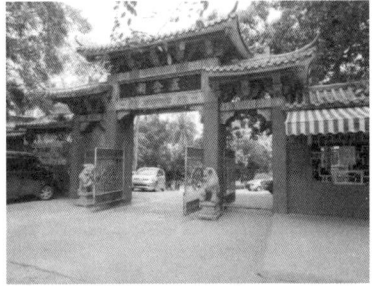

After many years of renovation and development, the existing Temple of Five Lords is now an attractive ancient architectural complex that mainly include the Five-Lord Temple, the Sugong Temple, Fubo temples, Guanjiatang Hall and Xueputang Hall. They cover an area of about 2,800 square meters.

The Five-Lord Temple, or No. 1 Building in Hainan, is the main part of this building complex even though it is only a two-storied wooden building. It was constructed to commemorate the five famous officials—Li Deyu, Li Gang, Zhao Ding, Li Guang and Hu Quan who were banished to Hainan during the Tang Dynasty (618 – 907) and the Song Dynasty (960 – 1279). The main hall houses the lifelike stone statues of the five prestigious officials. On the inner pillars, there

are two couplets. Additionally, a stone tablet that was carved with calligraphy inscriptions of Emperor Huizong in the Song Dynasty, has also been displayed in the temple.

Sugong Temple, located in the east of the Five-Lord Temple, is another fascinating destination. Su Dongpo was one of the greatest poets of the Song Dynasty. He was active in promoting local education despite his banishment. He volunteered to dig two wells for the locals when he heard that they were difficult in getting water supplies. Hence the local people constructed a temple to commemorate his contributions to their community. One of the wells still exists until now.

On the right of the Five-Lord Temple, there is a peaceful yard where fresh flowers and thriving trees are planted. There are two main buildings here. One is the Xueputang Hall where the famous scholar Guo Wanxiang gave lectures. The other is Monastery of Five Lords where the local students in the Qing Dynasty learned historical works and poems.

If you want to know more about the famous people in the history of Hainan Province, you can visit the museum which will definitely fulfill your appetite for knowledge.

Notes:

1. The Five-Lord Temple, located in Haifu Road, was originally constructed during the reign of Emperor Wanli in the Ming Dynasty.

位于海府路的五公祠，原为明代万历皇帝在位期间建造的。

2. After many years of renovation and development, the existing Temple of Five Lords is now an attractive ancient architectural complex that mainly include the Five-

Lord Temple, the Sugong Temple, Fubo temples, Guanjiatang Hall and Xueputang Hall.

历经过多年的修缮和发展，五公祠现在是一个引人入胜的古建筑群，主要包括五公祠、苏公祠、伏波祠、观稼堂、学圃堂。

3. It was constructed to commemorate the five famous officials—Li Deyu, Li Gang, Zhao Ding, Li Guang and Hu Quan who were banished to Hainan during the Tang Dynasty (618 –907) and the Song Dynasty (960 –1279).

建造五公祠原是为了纪念五位著名官员——李德裕、李刚、赵鼎、李光和胡铨，他们分别在唐代（公元618—907 年）和宋代（公元960—1279 年）被流放到海南。

4. Additionally, a stone tablet that was carved with calligraphy inscriptions of Emperor Huizong in the Song Dynasty, has also been displayed in the temple.

此外，刻有宋代徽宗帝的书法碑文也陈列在五公祠内。

5. Hence the local people constructed a temple to commemorate his contributions to their community.

于是，当地人建造了一座公祠来纪念他对当地的贡献。

Chapter 3 Shishan Volcanic Cluster National Geopark

Shishan Volcanic Cluster National Geopark is located just 15 kilometers from the city center and gives a great insight into the early formation of Hainan Island. The park covers 180 square kilometers and consists of over 40 Quaternary volcanoes with a number of lava landscapes and up to 30 volcanic rocks.

The eruption of the ancient Qiongbei Volcano left the most intact volcano craters here. According to geologists, the latest eruption happened about 13,000 years ago, and now, 36 relics of the craters can be seen here. Among them the highest one is the Saddle Hill which is about 222.8 meters high.

There are stone stairs leading to the top of the hill as well as the bottom of the volcano crater. On a clear day, you can have a bird's-eye view of the picturesque Haikou. Once you reach the top, you can descend from the various paths to the caves inside the extinct volcano, where you can explore the mystery of volcano eruption.

The park was awarded Geopark status by the United Nations Educational,

Scientific and Cultural Organization. Today, the park is equipped with the volcano cultural garden, ecological garden, the green corridor, and the crater's garden, attracting visitors from both home and abroad. You can also enjoy the rustic flavor of the local people, taste the delicious food, and purchase the local handiwork too.

Notes：

1. Shishan Volcanic Cluster National Geopark is located just 15 kilometers from the city center and gives a great insight into the early formation of Hainan Island.

石山火山群国家地质公园距市中心仅 15 公里，它有助于考察海南岛早期的形成。

2. The eruption of the ancient Qiongbei Volcano left the most intact volcano craters here.

古老的琼北火山喷发在这里留下最完整的火山口。

3. On a clear day, you can have a bird's-eye view of the picturesque Haikou.

天气晴朗的时候，您可以鸟瞰景色如画的海口市。

4. Once you reach the top, you can descend from the various paths to the caves inside the extinct volcano, where you can explore the mystery of volcano eruption.

一旦您到达山顶，就可以在死火山山洞内沿着不同的路走到洞底，探索火山爆发的奥秘。

5. Today, the park is equipped with the volcano cultural garden, ecological garden, the green corridor, and the crater's garden, attracting visitors from both home and abroad.

今天，公园拥有火山文化园、生态园、绿色走廊和火山口花园，吸引了来自国内外的游客。

Chapter 4 Dongzhai Harbor Mangrove Natural Reserve Area

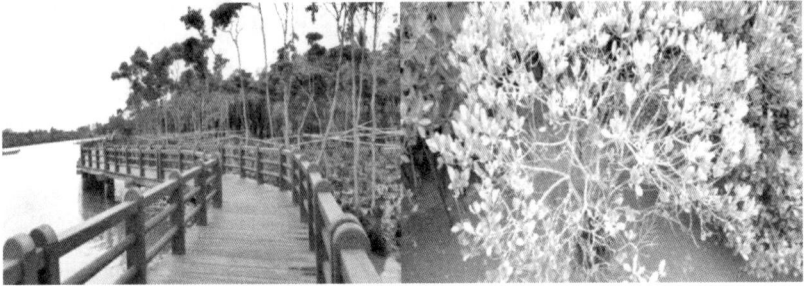

Known for the largest and the first mangrove natural reserve area in China, Dongzhai Harbor is located in the northeast of Haikou with an area of 3,337.6 hectares. It is a typical tropical jungle, and the mangrove tree family can be seen everywhere in the area. Mangrove is a kind of tropical tree that grows in swamps and sends roots down from its branches. When the tide is high, the mangroves are submerged by the water, and leave only the green crowns for people to wonder at their marvelous nature.

Dongzhai Harbor Mangrove Natural Reserve Area is also called "heaven for birds". About 159 species of birds inhabit the reserve, including many rare migratory birds. So, it is not only a national mangrove reserve, but also a wetland of international importance especially as a waterfowl habitat. Winter is the best season for bird watching as tens of thousands of birds migrate here for food. Because of the nourishment the mangroves provide to the swamp, marine animals prefer to spawn and raise their infants here. Fish, shrimp and shellfish in abundance can fill visitors' stomach freshly and palatably, and provide a substantial feast for the birds.

Apart from the beautiful scenery, there are ruins in the harbor: villages in the sea. Historical records say that at midnight on July 13th, 1605, a severe earthquake occurred and made 72 villages subside into the sea. Hundreds of years later, the 72 villages have become an amazing underwater sight waiting for visitors to discover their extraordinary story.

No matter what kind of adventure you are looking for, whether natural sightings of the mangroves and birds, or the underwater sightseeing, or you just want to have a good meal of local delicacy, you can certainly have a good time in Dongzhai Harbor Mangrove Nature Reserve Area.

Notes:

1. It is a typical tropical jungle, and the mangrove tree family can be seen everywhere in the area.

这是一个典型的热带丛林,红树科植物在这个地区随处可见。

2. Mangrove is a kind of tropical tree that grows in swamps and sends roots down from its branches.

红树林是生长在沼泽中的一种热带树,根部从树枝上垂下来。

3. So, it is not only a national mangrove reserve, but also a wetland of international importance especially as a waterfowl habitat.

因此,它不仅是一个国家级红树林保护区,也是世界级重要湿地,尤其是水禽栖息地。

4. Because of the nourishment the mangroves provide to the swamp, marine animals prefer to spawn and raise their infants here.

由于红树林供给沼泽地营养,海洋动物更喜欢在这里产卵并哺育它们的雏儿。

5. Historical records say that at midnight on July 13th, 1605, a severe earthquake occurred and made 72 villages subside into the sea.

历史记载说，1605 年 7 月 13 日午夜，一场强烈的地震发生，使得 72 个村庄沉入大海。

Chapter 5 Holiday Beach Resort

Holiday Beach is a major recreational resort in the west of Haikou. It is a typical place for touring and having leisure at the beach. The Holiday Beach is located at the side of Binhai Road off the west coast, and its total length is 6 kilometers long, covering a total area of 54 hectares. It is 11 kilometers away from the downtown area, providing sunbathing, swimming, water sports and seafood restaurant services for the visitors home and abroad. Now it has become a recreational tourism attraction that combines natural landscapes and man-made scenery, featuring an international beach city, where you can enjoy the fine views of the sparkling waters of the ocean, the sun-setting, the coconut trees, the warm sunshine and the blue sky. The whole beach can be divided into four areas: sun bath area on the beach, sport area in the sea, sea food area and holiday area.

"Holiday Beach" was named by Xia Luping, a researcher from Hainan Provincial Party School. Mr. Xia got inspired from Hilton Beach Resort at Hawaiian Waikiki Beach when he was touring there. The name "Holiday Beach" means to be a good place for city people to spend their holidays as well as to lead a leisure lifestyle in Haikou.

An unusual feature of the Holiday Beach Resort is the "kissing fish". These fishes can live happily in 40℃ water, and they will nibble at your body to provide delightful underwater skin-cleansing care.

Beach barbecue is the best choice for tourists in summer. Every weekend, there are always several people gathering together on the beach. They are either enjoying the beautiful scenery, or sharing the food barbecued together.

Summer is the best season to come to Holiday Beach when you can swim in the sea. If you come here in spring or autumn, you can enjoy the good weather but not the seawater.

So welcome to Holiday Beach, just off Binhai Road, Haikou. It awaits you!

Notes：

1. The Holiday Beach is located at the side of Binhai Road off the west coast, and its total length is 6 kilometers long, covering a total area of 54 hectares.

假日海滩位于滨海路一侧的西海岸沿岸，全长6公里，占地总面积54公顷。

2. It is 11 kilometers away from the downtown area, providing sunbathing, swimming, water sports and seafood restaurant services for the visitors home and abroad.

它距市区11公里，为国内外的游客提供日光浴、游泳、水上运动和海鲜餐厅服务。

3. Mr. Xia got inspired from Hilton Beach Resort at Hawaiian Waikiki Beach when he was touring there.

夏先生取名的灵感来自于他住过的夏威夷威基基海滩上的希尔顿假日酒店。

4. These fishes can live happily in 40℃ water, and they will nibble at your body to provide delightful underwater skin-cleansing care.

这些鱼可以在40度的水中快乐地生活，它们会轻咬人们的表皮，提供令人愉悦的水下皮肤清洁护理。

5. Beach barbecue is the best choice for tourists in summer.

海滩烧烤是夏季游客的最佳选择。

Chapter 6   Qilou Arcades

Located in the downtown of Haikou, Qilou Arcades feature a stylish integration of European and Asian architectures, as well as Indian and Arabic influences. With delicately carved window frame and doors, and western-style Roman columns and arches, the Qilou buildings form the city's most exotic landscapes.

The history of Qilou Arcades could be dated back to the late of 1800s when Haikou opened its door and became a commercial port due to the signing of Tianjin Treaty. Later, the Haikou Custom was set up. Many countries like U. K. , France and Germany established consulates in Haikou, which gradually grew into a booming modern city and a commercial hub trading with South East Asia. At that time, its well-developed sea transportation network connected Haikou to Bangkok, Kuala Lumpur, Singapore, Saigon, Haiphong, Hong Kong, Xiamen, Taiwan, Guangzhou, Beihai and so on. Going back and forth between Hainan and South East Asia or the coastal area of mainland, Hainan businessmen brought architectural elements from different places back to Haikou, giving the city an exotic look.

Based on historical record, the first Qilou building in Haikou was built in 1894 at

Sipailou Street, which is now called North Bo' ai Street. Historically, the street has housed consulates, churches, post offices, banks and chambers of commerce belonging to 13 different countries. Standing between two and four stories in height, Qilou has its ground floor set back halfway into the building so that it can be used as a storefront to take shelter from rain and sunlight. The upper floors serve as the living quarters, and extend over the pavement supported by columns.

Qilou buildings now can be mainly found on Zhongshan Road, South Xinhua Road, East Jiefang Road, Bo' ai Road and Deshengsha Road. In total, there are more than 200 Qilou buildings in the streets.

Today, it remains Haikou' s business center while giving you a taste of traditional life of Haikou. Salesmen in the shops, passers-by taking shelter from the rain, vendors having a short break, yelling hucksters, and young girls shopping along the street with hands in hands...you can see all these lively images in Qilou Arcades.

Undoubtedly, Qilou Arcades Street is a lively history book of Haikou, and it was selected as one of the 10 Historical and Cultural Streets of China in 2007.

Notes:

1. Located in the downtown of Haikou, Qilou Arcades feature a stylish integration of European and Asian architectures, as well as Indian and Arabic influences.

坐落于海口的骑楼老街既具有欧亚建筑风格，又受到印度和阿拉伯风格的影响。

2. At that time, its well-developed sea transportation network connected Haikou to Bangkok, Kuala Lumpur, Singapore, Saigon, Haiphong, Hong Kong, Xiamen, Taiwan, Guangzhou, Beihai and so on.

当时发达的海上交通网络将海口与曼谷，吉隆坡，新加坡，西贡，海防，香港，厦门，台湾，广州，北海等城市连接起来。

3. Historically, the street has housed consulates, churches, post offices, banks and chambers of commerce belonging to 13 different countries.

历史上，这条街曾驻有 13 个不同国家的领事馆、教堂、邮局、银行和商会。

4. Salesmen in the shops, passers-by taking shelter from the rain, vendors having a short break, yelling hucksters, and young girls shopping along the street with hands in hands...you can see all these lively images in Qilou Arcades.

商店里的售货员，躲避风雨的路人，稍作休息的小商贩，吆喝的小贩，和手牵手逛街的年轻姑娘……在骑楼老街随处可见这些生动的街景。

5. Undoubtedly, Qilou Arcades Street is a lively history book of Haikou, and it was selected as one of the 10 Historical and Cultural Streets of China in 2007.

毫无疑问，骑楼老街是海口市的一本生动的历史书。它在 2007 年被评为"中国 10 大历史文化名街"之一。

Chapter 7　Hairui Tomb

Hairui Tomb was built to commemorate this upright official and now it is one of the key historical sites at the Binya Village, Xiuying District of Haikou. Hairui was born in Qiongshan and known as an official who was free from corruption in the Ming Dynasty.

The tomb was built in 1589 and it is said that when people was carrying Hairui's coffin, suddenly the rope broke, so people considered that this must be the very place where Hairui himself had chosen to be his place. Hairui Tomb covers an area of 7.4 acres and all the architectures around this tomb form a solemn, simple and unsophisticated style.

In the middle, there is a high archway on which four scarlet Chinese characters "Yue Dong Zheng Qi" were written.

The grave path was paved with granite and there are three memorials on the way. On the sides of the path leading to the tomb, there stands stone statue shaped like sheep, horses, lions, tortures, and human beings. Hairui Tomb was completely built by granite, with a round top, six-angled base, a height of 3 meters, and a reducing size from up to down, thus it looks like an ancient bell. Different kinds of evergreen trees are planted around the cemetery, such as coconut trees, pines, and cypresses. Hairui Cultural Exhibit Hall is also the place where visitors can pay their respect.

Notes:

1. Hairui was born in Qiongshan and known as an official who was free from corruption in the Ming Dynasty.

海瑞出生于琼山，是明代著名的清官。

2. The tomb was built in 1589 and it is said that when people was carrying Hairui's coffin, suddenly the rope broke, so people considered that this must be the very place where Hairui himself had chosen to be his place.

墓地建于1589年，据说当时人们抬着海瑞的灵柩，突然绳子断了，所以人们认为这应该是海瑞自选的墓地。

3. In the middle, there is a high archway on which four scarlet Chinese characters "Yue Dong Zheng Qi" were written.

中间有一个高高的拱门，上面写着"粤东正气"四个红色大字。

4. Hairui Tomb was completely built by granite, with a round top, six-angled base, a height of 3 meters, and a reducing size from up to down, thus it looks like an ancient bell.

海瑞墓完全由花岗岩砌成，圆顶、六角形的基座，高三米，自上而下逐渐变窄，因此它看起来像一座古老的钟。

5. Hairui Cultural Exhibit Hall is also the place where visitors can pay their respect.

海瑞文化陈列馆也是游客瞻仰海瑞的地方。

Chapter 8　Feng Xiaogang Movie Town

Movie Town is a collaboration among Mission Hills Group, film director Feng Xiaogang, and, Huayi Brothers Media Corporation. Being the first of its kind in China, it integrates the beauty of architecture, film and retail into a unique tourist destination.

Located at Mission Hills, Haikou, the Movie Town features architectures inspired by settings from Director Feng's most popular movies, such as "Back to 1942" "Tangshan Earthquake" and "If You Are the One". It aims to build an all-inclusive entertainment and commercial tourism district, showcasing how China's landscape has evolved over the past century.

The attractions in the Movie Town include key districts— "1942 Street" "Nanyang Street" and "Ancient Beijing Street"; Church and Square, Park View Area, Avenue of Stars, and the world's largest Movie Studio covering 8,000 square meters providing complementary services.

1942 Street

The first phase of Movie Town features "1942 Street", depicting Republican Era buildings in Chongqing as featured in Feng's movie "Back to 1942". A total of 91 buildings showcase the different architectural styles which prevailed at the time, from the four cities along the Yangtze River: Chongqing, Wuhan, Nanjing and Shanghai. Of the 91 buildings, 20 have been restored exactly as they were in the old pictures, e.g. Xishan Bell Tower, Chongqing Cathay Theatre, and Shanghai Rongguang Theatre; each building with a long history evokes old memories.

Nanyang Street

Built on the bank of a river that is over 300 meters long, "Nanyang Street" has 70 buildings characterized by typical South Asian features, where the Chinese elements stand in contrast to western styles. The very appealing and intriguing ones are buildings that are representative of architectural styles from that period, like memorial arches, piers, bridges and churches.

Ancient Beijing Street

Buildings in the street mimic the styles of architectures from the 1950s to 1960s, after the People's Republic of China was founded. They are magnificent, dignified and austere; tourists may find traces of their growing up memories.

Church and Square

Inspired by European cities' urban planning with churches as the focus, the unique architectures here are decorated with exquisite carvings, designs and ornaments similar to that of churches in Europe. These buildings stand towering towards the sky, evoking a sense of solemness and respect.

Park View Area

Buildings in the area are designed according to the settings from Director Feng Xiaogang's movies for celebrating Chinese New Year, such as "If You Are the One" "The Banquet" "A World Without Thieves" "Tangshan Earthquake", with an aim to build a movie-themed park view area combining architectural arts, movie culture, commerce and entertainment.

Avenue of Stars

Walking on the Avenue of Stars, tourists can see autographs and handprints of 80 popular local and international celebrities, most of whom have visited Movie Town. It is a great fun to walk on the Avenue and feel the charm of these stars, with a possibility of meeting your idols in person.

The Movie Studio

The area holds several large movie studios with a combined area of 8,000 square meters, the largest in the world. The studios are equipped with a perfect set of facilities, as well as apartments for movie stars. It will be a place where Chinese movie stars gather and shine.

Notes:

1. Being the first of its kind in China, it integrates the beauty of architecture, film and retail into a unique tourist destination.

它是首次以导演命名、集建筑、影视和零售行业美于一体的独具特色的旅游胜地。

2. Located at Mission Hills, Haikou, the Movie Town features architectures inspired by settings from Director Feng's most popular movies, such as "Back to 1942" "Tangshan Earthquake" and "If You Are the One".

电影公社位于海口观澜湖，建筑特色的灵感来自于冯小刚导演最受欢迎的电影场景，如《1942》《唐山大地震》和《非诚勿扰》。

3. A total of 91 buildings showcase the different architectural styles which prevailed at the time, from the four cities along the Yangtze River: Chongqing, Wuhan, Nanjing and Shanghai.

共有91座建筑展示了当时盛行的长江沿岸四个城市——重庆、武汉、南京和上海的不同建筑风格。

4. Inspired by European cities' urban planning with churches as the focus, the unique architectures here are decorated with exquisite carvings, designs and ornaments similar to that of churches in Europe.

受到欧洲城市以教堂为中心的城市规划启发，这里建筑物的雕刻独特，设计和装饰都很精致，和欧洲教堂很像。

5. Walking on the Avenue of Stars, tourists can see autographs and handprints of 80 popular local and international celebrities, most of whom have visited Movie Town.

走在星光大道上，游客可以看到80位国内外名人的签名和手印，他们大部分都曾参观过电影公社。

Part Ⅲ Sanya (1)

This part will focus on...

· general Introduction to Sanya;

· Yalong Bay National Holiday Resort;

· Tianya Haijiao Scenic Area;

· Sanya Dongtian Park;

· West Island Marine Cultural Tourism Area;

· Wuzhizhou Island;

· Dadonghai Beach;

· Yalong Bay Tropical Paradise Forest Park.

Chapter 1 General Introduction to Sanya

Sanya is a famous coastal tourist city with tropical landscapes and special local customs, and it is the most important economic, cultural and foreign trade port in the southern part of Hainan. Situated on the southern tip of Hainan Island, its latitude is almost the same as Hawaii. Therefore, it's often called "the Hawaii of China" or "Oriental Hawaii".

Sanya is a very convenient place for exchange with countries in Southeast Asia because of its location. It is also an important sea route connecting China with Southwest Asia, Africa and Europe. With a coastline of 209.1 kilometers, it consists of 10 islands and 19 harbors. And the Sanya Harbor has now become an important port of export for deluxe passengers' ships and for trade with foreign countries. In addition, Sanya Phoenix International Airport, the second largest airport in Hainan Province, serves flights to domestic and foreign cities.

Sanya is a world-famous tropical seashore tour-enjoying city. It enjoys clean sea water, fresh air, beautiful beaches and bright sunshine and is rich in natural tropical scenery and historical sites. Its tourist attractions include Yalong Bay National Holiday Resort, Dadonghai Tourist Zone, Tianya Haijiao, Luhuitou Park, Nanshan Cultural and Tourist Zone, Wuzhizhou Island, Yalong Bay Tropical Paradise Forest Park, etc. Local specialties include handicrafts made of seashells, horn-ware, coconut shell carving products, squid and pepper, etc.

In recent years, thanks to an increasing flow of tourism, Sanya now has over one hundred luxury hotels, with an annual reception capacity over 10 million people. Sheraton, Hilton, Marriott, and Ritz-Carlton are just some of the names of intercontinental hotel chains that have settled in Sanya's tourist resort area.

The Hainan Carnival, which annually attracts both locals and travelers from near and far, creates a carnival atmosphere covering the whole of Hainan Island, with a variety of events and exhibitions happening throughout the Carnival period. Sanya and Haikou are the main venues for the carnival in 2017. To encourage more potential participants to come out and enjoy this year's events, there are many main festival events planned for Sanya, including: the 67th Miss World Finals, Sanya Destination

Wedding Expo, the 21st Tianya Haijiao International Wedding Festival, 2017 "Silk Road" International Cultural Arts Festival, 2017 2nd Sanya International Cultural Industry Fair, China Rendez-Vous 2017, 2017 Youth Sailing World Championships, etc. Sanya has been embraced by beauties worldwide, and has shown the world its beauty and charm.

Notes:

1. Sanya is a famous coastal tourist city with tropical landscapes and special local customs, and it is the most important economic, cultural and foreign trade port in the southern part of Hainan.

三亚是一个风景优美、风情独特的滨海旅游城市，是海南南部最重要的经济、文化和对外贸易港口。

2. And the Sanya Harbor has now become an important port of export for deluxe passengers' ships and for trade with foreign countries.

三亚港现已成为豪华邮轮和对外贸易的重要出口口岸。

3. Its tourist attractions include Yalong Bay National Holiday Resort, Dadonghai Tourist Zone, Tianya Haijiao, Luhuitou Park, Nanshan Cultural and Tourist Zone, Wuzhizhou Island, Yalong Bay Tropical Paradise Forest Park, etc.

旅游景点包括亚龙湾国家假日度假酒店、大东海旅游区、天涯海角、鹿回头山顶公园、南山文化旅游区、蜈支洲岛、亚龙湾热带天堂森林公园等。

4. Sheraton, Hilton, Marriott, and Ritz-Carlton are just some of the names of intercontinental hotel chains that have settled in Sanya's tourist resort area.

喜来登、希尔顿、万豪和丽思卡尔顿都是入驻三亚旅游度假区的国际连锁酒店。

5. To encourage more potential participants to come out and enjoy this year's events, there are many main festival events planned for Sanya, including: the 67th Miss World Finals, Sanya Destination Wedding Expo, the 21st Tianya Haijiao International Wedding Festival, 2017 "Silk Road" International Cultural Arts

Festival, 2017 2nd Sanya International Cultural Industry Fair, China Rendez-Vous 2017, 2017 Youth Sailing World Championships, etc.

为了鼓励更多潜在的参与者加入并享受这一年的盛事，许多主要节庆活动都策划在三亚举行，包括：第 67 届世界小姐总决赛，三亚目的地婚礼博览会，第 21 届天涯海角国际婚庆节，2017 "丝绸之路" 国际文化艺术节，2017 第二届三亚国际文化产业博览会，2017 中国海天盛筵，2017 青少年帆船世界锦标赛等。

Chapter 2   Yalong Bay National Holiday Resort

Thanks to the perfect position, Yalong Bay is the premier destination for fun in Sanya with features of undulating green hills, clear seawater, soft sandy beach, and pleasant climate in all seasons. It provides you with an irresistible combination of a world-class beach, matchless swimming and diving, international resorts and superb golf facilities in one extraordinary package.

Yalong Bay centers on a crescent-shaped beach with its beach length of 2 times than that of Hawaii. The sea off the beach is so clear that visibility can reach almost eight meters, making it ideal for divers to enjoy the nearby coral reefs. Those who prefer lounging in the swimming pool while overlooking the sea will find pools of every size in the international resorts now. More resorts are planned like Sheraton, Shangri-La, and Hyatt.

"No sea deserves a look other than Sanya; no bay deserves a true bay except Yalong." Yalong Bay is arguably Hainan's best beach and definitely the most pristine.

There are 7 kilometers of white sand stretches along the clean, blue water here, backed by palm trees and lush green hills. This is a marine reserve under protection and commercial fishing is forbidden here, keeping the water very clean and lovely for swimming.

Facilities are also good here. This great beach is adjacent to shops, restaurants and a museum with a large collection of sea shells. There is also a charming outdoor butterfly garden with a mountain hiking trail and some great walks. Hot springs, numerous golf courses and submarine cruises are also offered.

In addition to sunshine, beaches, watersports and golf, Yalong Bay is graced with odd rocks, grotesque shoals and idyllic views. For ventures of rock climbing and hiking among a wide selection of activities and attractions, prime locations are Jinmu Cape and Yalong Cape. Within the bay there are five islands with Boar Island in the center, Dongzhou and Xizhou in the south, Dongpai and Xipai in the west. The other attractions in Yalong Bay include the Central Square, the Sea Shell Museum and Butterfly Valley.

The 1,000 square meters of Butterfly Valley is filled with vibrant colorful butterflies flying around. In the Butterfly Valley, an open air flight cage will ensure that visitors are able to interact closely with butterflies. In the large-scale exhibition hall, there are over 2,000 kinds of specimens of butterflies and insects on display. The valley also displays some of China's most rare and precious butterflies, including Peking Papilio.

Yalong Bay is definitely a paradise for holidays.

Notes:

1. Thanks to the perfect position, Yalong Bay is the premier destination for fun in Sanya with features of undulating green hills, clear seawater, soft sandy beach, and pleasant climate in all seasons.

亚龙湾地理位置优越，是三亚旅游的首选目的地，山峦起伏，海水清澈，沙滩柔软，四季气候宜人。

2. The sea off the beach is so clear that visibility can reach almost eight meters, making it ideal for divers to enjoy the nearby coral reefs.

近海海水非常清澈，能见度几乎可达八米，非常适合潜水者观赏附近的珊瑚礁。

3. This is a marine reserve under protection and commercial fishing is forbidden here, keeping the water very clean and lovely for swimming.

这里是一个受保护的海洋保护区，禁止商业捕鱼，以保持水的清洁和游泳的乐趣。

4. For ventures of rock climbing and hiking among a wide selection of activities and attractions, prime locations are Jinmu Cape and Yalong Cape. Within the bay there are five islands with Boar Island in the center, Dongzhou and Xizhou in the south, Dongpai and Xipai in the west.

锦母角和亚龙角是攀崖探险活动的良好场所。湾内共有五个岛屿，海面上以野猪岛为中心，南有东洲岛、西洲岛，西有东排、西排。

5. The other attractions in Yalong Bay include the Central Square, the Sea Shell Museum and Butterfly Valley.

亚龙湾的其他景点包括中心广场、贝壳博物馆和蝴蝶谷。

Chapter 3 Tianya Haijiao Scenic Area

Tianya Haijiao literally means "the end of the sky and the corner of the sea" and it is a scenic spot located at the southwest seaside of Sanya. The scenic spot covers a land area of 10. 4 square kilometers and a sea area of 6 square kilometers. It is famous for its charming sea-view and ethnic customs. What's more, visitors can be fascinated by the giant rocks, coral reefs, coconut tree forest, sea waves, sea gulls and clouds.

Well-being Rock

The Tianya Rock is also known as Well-being Rock. When looked at it from the distance, this rock looks like a mountain along the coast of the South China Sea. When looked at it from a closer spot, the rock is giant and square. A long history can be dated back to the Qing Dynasty when Cheng Zhe, the mayor of Yazhou, inscribed two Chinese characters—Tian Ya on the rock, in hope of gaining the blessing for the well-being of the people and the state.

The Lucky Rock

The Haijiao Rock is also known as the Lucky Rock. The fishermen nearby consider it as a beacon for the fishery. In the past, there was a rock climbing competition among fishermen. It was said that the one who could first reach the top of this rock would catch big fishes first. On January 8th of 1938, Mr. Wang Yi, the military commander of Hainan, visited the place during the Anti-Japanese War. He saw the Tianya Rock, and noticed that there was no

Haijiao Rock. Then he saw the rock with a sharp and tall tip, so he ordered people to inscribe two Chinese characters—Hai Jiao on it.

Fortune Rock

The "Nantian yizhu" Rock Column is like a giant stick pointing to the sky. It symbolizes vitality and vigor. The local people call it as the Fortune Rock or Prosperity Rock. The view of this rock is so impressive that it has been printed on the banknote of two-yuan for the fourth set of RMB. The inscription of Nantian yizhu was written by Fan Yuntian, the mayor of Yazhou in 1909 in the Qing Dynasty.

Romance Rock

In the sea, there is a heart-shaped rock which is known as the Romance Rock. Two Chinese characters "sun" and "moon" were inscribed respectively on each side of the rock. There is a legend for this rock. Long long ago, a young man and a young girl fell in love with each other, but they came from two feuding families. Because of the opposition of both families, they had to run to the seaside for a free life, but both families heard the news and chased after them. They had no choice but to jump into the sea and changed into one huge rock floating on the surface of the water. Later, this heart-shaped rock has also been called "Man and Wife Rock", symbolizing their faithful love.

With the construction and development of the scenic area, Tianya Haijiao has a more modern, romantic and fashion environment. It is the terminal of the first transmission of torch relay of 2008 Beijing Olympics in Sanya. And the large-scale celebrating evening party held in the front of "Tianya" rock has made Tianya Haijiao Scenic Area well-known in the world. The large scale activities such as "Tianya Haijiao International Wedding Festival" and "New Silk Road Model Contest" have been held here too. Therefore, Tianya Haijiao Scenic Area has become the holy place for lovers expressing their love and the models showing their beautiful charm.

Tianya Haijiao Scenic Area has attracted tourists from all over the world every year to realize their dreams of "Going around the end of the earth". The song "Please Come to Tianya Haijiao" has been sung all over the country which has made Tianya Haijiao scenic spot the symbol of Sanya. Tourists may not only enjoy a tropical seaside resort, but also can experience its culture and custom. Of course, the most unique view is the five famous rocks standing on the seashore and the inscriptions on them.

Notes：

1. Tianya Haijiao literally means "the end of the sky and the corner of the sea" and it is a scenic spot located at the southwest seaside of Sanya.

"天涯海角" 意为 "天之涯，海之角"，是位于三亚西南部海滨的一个风景区。

2. A long history can be dated back to the Qing Dynasty when Cheng Zhe, the mayor of Yazhou, inscribed two Chinese characters—Tian Ya on the rock, in hope of gaining the blessing for the well-being of the people and the state.

悠久的历史可以追溯到清代，当时崖州知州程哲在岩石上题刻了 "天涯" 二字，祈求国家与人民的福祉。

3. It is the terminal of the first transmission of torch relay of 2008 Beijing Olympics in Sanya.

它是 2008 年北京奥运会火炬传递在三亚首传的终点站。

4. The large scale activities such as "Tianya Haijiao International Wedding Festival" and "New Silk Road Model Contest" have been held here too.

"天涯海角国际婚庆节"和"新丝路模特大赛"等大型赛事也在此举行。

5. The song "Please Come to Tianya Haijiao" has been sung all over the country which has made Tianya Haijiao scenic spot the symbol of Sanya.

一曲《请到天涯海角来》传唱大江南北，使得"天涯海角"风景区成为三亚的标志。

Chapter 4 Sanya Dongtian Park

Sanya Dongtian Park is a scenic attraction famous for the longest history in Hainan, which was founded in the South Song Dynasty (1187). As one of the first national 5A tourist attractions, it has been known as "The 800-year-old No. 1 Scenic Spot in Hainan" from the ancient time. Situated at 40 kilometers west of Sanya, this park boasts seas, mountains, rocks and caves of special beauty.

Currently, over one million tourists visit this park every year. Combined with ancient Yazhou culture, Dongtian Park has become an international tourist attraction with traditional Chinese culture, mixing coastal scenery, custom and leisure vacation together.

Sanya Dongtian Park has enjoyed over 800 years of history since it was developed in the Song Dynasty, so it is the earliest developed scenic attraction in the history of Hainan. The graceful scenery consisting of mountains, seas, rocks, and woods has attracted countless poets and celebrities

to visit here. Such protected cultural relics as "Fishing Platform" "The Minor Grotto Heaven" "Wonders of the Sea and the Hills", and "Shou" Stele etc. had been recorded and chanted by poets in previous dynasties. In the modern time, even Guo Moruo, and Jiang Zemin left their poems here. So it is a famous tourist attraction under protection and historical interests in Hainan.

The Minor Grotto Heaven, *Xiaodongtian* in Chinese was formed by rocky ledges along the sea, like a stone chamber or a cave. The walls are smooth, the area is more than 20 squares, and the depth is 28 meters. The ancients said, "Immortal cave looks like a cave but is not a cave." There is a "Fishing Platform" next to Xiao Dongtian. According to legend, it is a chair for an immortal old man to fish the "Six Huge Legendary Turtles".

Dongtian Park scattered thirty thousand "Nanshan Old Pines". This kind of tree looks like pines, but is not. It is called Dracaena Draco, a rare national tree species under second class protection. Its resin can be used as medicine for hemostasis and promoting granulation. Roots and branches of those thirty thousand trees are intertwined with each other, like old long-lived people sitting cross-legged. The oldest is at least five to six thousand years old. Those trees together with the treasured place fully express the eternal blessing of "as long-lived as the Old Pines in Nanshan Mountain" and constitute a domestic unique natural and cultural wonder.

Bestowed by Empress Dowager Cixi, "Shou" Stele is one of the key protected cultural relics of Sanya, 2. 76 meters high, 1. 1 meters wide and 0. 3 meters thick. The Chinese character "Shou" is engraved in the center, 1. 45 meters high and 0. 68 meters wide. As recorded on *Yazhou Chorography*, "Shou" Stele was made in the 28th year of the Guangxu Period of the

Qing Dynasty (1902).

At that time, there was an official named Wang Gen who was good at painting. Emperor Guangxu appreciated his painting skills, and at Cixi' s 60th birthday, asked him to paint a screen for Cixi. His paintings were praised both by Cixi and Emperor Guangxu, so Cixi wrote a "Shou" and granted it to Wang Gen. In 1901, when appointed as magistrate of Yazhou, Wang Gen asked craftsmen to engrave the "Shou" on the stele, and built a hall named Tongshan to place the stele. Later, Tongshan Hall was destroyed, and the "Shou" Stele was moved to Sanya Dongtian Park.

Notes：

1. Combined with ancient Yazhou culture, Dongtian Park has become an international tourist attraction with traditional Chinese culture, mixing coastal scenery, custom and leisure vacation together.

融聚古崖州文化，大小洞天是一个富有中国传统文化的国际旅游胜地，集滨海风光、风俗、休闲度假于一体。

2. Such protected cultural relics as "Fishing Platform" "The Minor Grotto Heaven" "Wonders of the Sea and the Hills", and "Shou" Stele etc. had been recorded and chanted by poets in previous dynasties.

历史保护文物如"钓台""小洞天""海山奇观"和"寿字"碑等都被历代文人记载吟唱。

3. It is called Dracaena Draco, a rare national tree species under second class protection.

这种树被称为龙血树，一种珍稀濒危植物，属国家二级重点保护树种。

4. Those trees together with the treasured place fully express the eternal blessing of "as long-lived as the Old Pines in Nanshan Mountain" and constitute a domestic unique natural and cultural wonder.

龙血树和这块宝地充分表达了"寿比南山不老松"的永恒祝福，构成了国内独特的自然和文化奇迹。

5. Bestowed by Empress Dowager Cixi, "Shou" Stele is one of the key protected cultural relics of Sanya, 2.76 meters high, 1.1 meters wide and 0.3 meters thick.

慈禧太后御笔"寿"字碑是三亚重点保护文物之一, 高2.76米, 宽1.1米, 厚0.3米。

Chapter 5   West Island Marine Cultural Tourism Area

West Island, the second-largest island in Hainan Province, covers an area of 2.8 square kilometers, and it is 8 kilometers away from Sanya. Tourists can take a yacht to get to the island in 25 minutes.

West Island is known as Turtle Island or West Hawks-bill Island (a kind of large turtle) from local folklore. It is shaped like a hawks-bill, which is like a turtle living in tropical area. This island has long been home to fishing tribes for generations, but its idyllic surroundings of sandy beaches, rocky coves, and palm trees are now being discovered by domestic and foreign tourists alike.

The island is filled with white sandy beaches, fresh air and clean water. The surrounding area is also abundant with many different types of fish, many different sea shells and coral reefs. Scuba diving or snorkeling in this area is a great activity

for the entire family. West Island Recreational World also provides several other activities and has 46 square kilometers of space. It would be a good choice to wander along the bay after supper to feel the soft sea breeze and warm sea water, and view the sunset. As you walk along the bay, you can see the fishermen trawling and hear their working songs resounding to the skies.

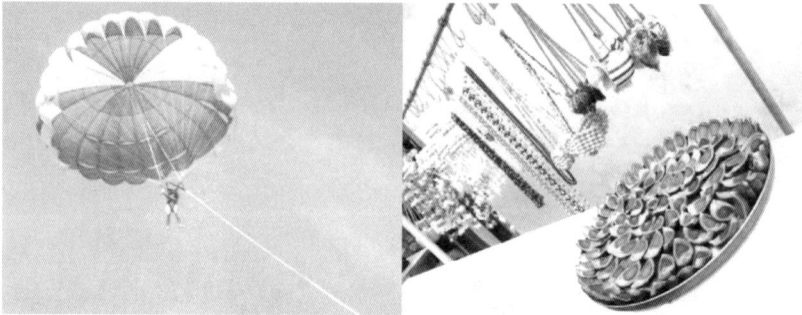

The island offers every kind of diversion for those with an active lifestyle. West Island boasts crystal clear waters with a wide array of marine life and extensive coral reefs to explore. Diving instructors are internationally (PADI) certified, and offer a full range of equipment for rental. Scuba excursions are available from shore or by boat. If you want an adrenaline rush, para-sailing, jet-skiing, and four-wheeling on beach ATVs are all available to test your mettle. If you just want to relax, take a break in the shade of the coconut trees, enjoy the tropical breeze, and savor the freshest of seafood at one of the island's restaurants.

West Island has a wide array of souvenirs to bring home for family and friends. Choosing from exotic seashells, beautiful coral pieces or minority handicrafts, you will end the trip with great satisfaction.

In short, this island is superb for indulging oneself on the beach and having a leisure time during a vacation.

Notes：

1. West Island, the second-largest island in Hainan Province, covers an area of 2.8 square kilometers, and it is 8 kilometers away from Sanya.

西岛是海南省第二大岛屿，面积2.8平方公里，距三亚8公里。

2. Tourists can take a yacht to get to the island in 25 minutes.

游客乘坐游艇，25分钟就可以到达岛上。

3. This island has long been home to fishing tribes for generations, but its idyllic surroundings of sandy beaches, rocky coves, and palm trees are now being discovered by domestic and foreign tourists alike.

这座岛原先是渔民世代打鱼之地，而如今岛四周的沙滩、峡谷、棕榈林等旖旎风光受到国内外游客青睐。

4. If you want an adrenaline rush, para-sailing, jet-skiing, and four-wheeling on beach ATVs are all available to test your mettle.

如果您想要刺激，拖曳伞、滑水、四轮沙滩车都可以测试您的勇气。

5. Choosing from exotic seashells, beautiful coral pieces or minority handicrafts, you will end the trip with great satisfaction.

您可以选择购买奇异的贝壳、美丽的珊瑚片或少数民族手工艺品，给这次旅行画上满意的句号。

Chapter 6   Wuzhizhou Island

Wuzhizhou Island in Haitang Bay has an area of 1. 48 square kilometers. With an irregular butterfly-like shape and a total coastline of 5. 7 kilometers, the island is about 30 kilometers to the northeast of Sanya.

The island was known as Guqizhou Island in ancient times and the earliest records could be dated back to the Qing Dynasty (1644 – 1911), when a temple was built to commemorate the originator of Chinese characters, Cang Jie. After the decline of the Qing Dynasty, the villagers rebuilt the temple to honor the Goddess Matsu, who had been believed to bestow good fortune on the local fishermen. From 1949 this island had become an important strategic defense zone. However, since the 1990s, the island began to play a completely new role as a romantic place in holiday and leisure.

As the island is in a tropical marine zone, the climate is temperate and pleasant all the year round. It is an ideal place for vacation, winter swimming as well as entertainment. There are over 2,700 plant varieties on the island, including the tall trees and dense bushes. The eastern and southern parts of the island are hilly and two high mountains connect to form a peak about 79. 9 meters high. In the west and north, the terrain is level. Soft white sand stretches as far as the eye can see beside a crystal clear blue sea, where protected coral reefs are rich in conches, sea urchins, sea cucumbers and tropical fishes of various colors.

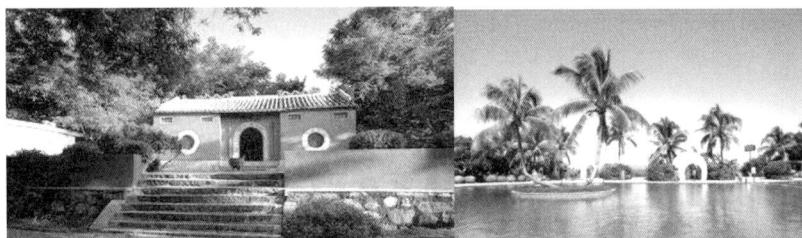

Besides Goddess Matsu Temple, there are many places of interest to visit including the Lover's Bridge, Sunrise Rock, the Gold Turtle Crawling toward the Sea, Lover's Island and the Life Well. The Sunrise Rock is the ideal spot for observing the sunrise. Apart from these natural sites, swimming pools, bars, gymnasiums and other places of entertainment are available in the northwest part of the island. For those who love extreme sports, local facilities include surfing, gliding, sailing and canoeing. For relaxation there is sun bathing and sea water bathing. In addition, Wuzhizhou Island is famous for scuba diving as coral reefs and brightly colored tropical fish abound in the warm water. Currently, only one third of the island has been developed.

In addition to the natural attractions of the island, tourists are certain to be pleased by the delightful catering facilities here. In the south of the island there are the Buffet Lunch Restaurant, the Pirate Bar, the Seafood Pool and the Chinese Restaurant all providing excellent food. The Summer Western Food Restaurant in the east corner and the Winter Western Food Restaurant in the west corner of the island also offer a choice of delicious food. Great seafood just caught locally such as lobsters, prawns, crabs, conch, sea cucumbers and jellyfish will make your mouth water! Furthermore, this island is rich in fruits so bananas, coconuts, mangos and other tropical fruits are plentiful and inexpensive.

For those who want to spend a night on the island, Wuzhizhou Island Holiday Center offers 81 guest rooms with a choice of perfect facilities. In addition, there are other choices available, like offshore log Cabin and the Presidents' Villa on the southern seashore; moreover, deluxe mountain-view rooms and sea-view rooms in wooden buildings are also very pleasant. In short, all the rooms have views of the fine scenery of the island.

Notes：

1. With an irregular butterfly-like shape and a total coastline of 5. 7 kilometers, the island is about 30 kilometers to the northeast of Sanya.

蜈支洲岛呈不规则的蝴蝶状，海岸线总长5. 7公里，距离三亚市东北部约30公里。

2. After the decline of the Qing Dynasty, the villagers rebuilt the temple to honor the Goddess Matsu, who had been believed to bestow good fortune on the local fishermen.

清政府衰败后，村民们重建了寺庙，供奉保佑当地渔民的妈祖。

3. Besides Goddess Matsu Temple, there are many places of interest to visit including the Lover's Bridge, Sunrise Rock, the Gold Turtle Crawling toward the Sea, Lover's Island and the Life Well.

除了妈祖庙外，还有许多值得游览的地方，包括情人桥、观日岩、金龟探海、情人岛和生命井。

4. In addition, Wuzhizhou Island is famous for scuba diving as coral reefs and brightly colored tropical fish abound in the warm water.

此外，蜈支洲岛以潜水闻名，因为温暖的海水中有许多珊瑚礁和色彩鲜艳的热带鱼。

5. In addition, there are other choices available, like offshore log Cabin and the Presidents' Villa on the southern seashore; moreover, deluxe mountain-view rooms and sea-view rooms in wooden buildings are also very pleasant.

此外，还有别的选择，如临海木屋、南滨总统别墅，而且豪华山景房和海景木屋也都非常舒适。

Chapter 7 Dadonghai Beach

Situated at the eastern area of Sanya, Dadonghai Tourist Zone is a nature-made and half-moon shaped shallow bay. It has enjoyed great popularity among tourists as it is close to the downtown of the city.

In this area, the beach is flat and the sea water is clean. And there are a lot of coast oaks along the bank and seashells scattering all over the sands. Its water temperature in winter is between 18℃ to 22℃, so it is an ideal place for winter holiday and one of the best places for diving, swimming and sunbath. It is entitled by the state tourism office as one of the "forty-best" tourist attractions in China.

With all spring-like seasons, Dadonghai is a top option for swimming; in addition, water sports and beach activities are at your services. Bathing in the warm sunshine and feeling the soft sea wind, you can enjoy yourself to the most just as you are part of the nature.

The beach's close proximity to the city means that it can get very busy but this still remains a pleasant and convenient spot to kick off your shoes, soak up in the sun and swim in the sea.

Facilities here are good too. There are numerous small restaurants and bars serving up tasty snacks and drinks. It is particularly pleasant here in the evenings, when the sun sets and the crowds disperse.

Notes：

1. Situated at the eastern area of Sanya, Dadonghai Tourist Zone is a nature-made and half-moon shaped shallow bay.

大东海旅游区位于三亚市东部地区，是一个天然的、半月形浅水湾。

2. It is entitled by the state tourism office as one of the "forty-best" tourist attractions in China.

它被国家旅游局列为中国"四十个最佳"的旅游景点之一。

3. With all spring-like seasons, Dadonghai is a top option for swimming; in addition, water sports and beach activities are at your services.

四季如春的大东海是游泳的首选地，此外，这里还提供水上运动和沙滩活动的服务。

4. The beach's close proximity to the city means that it can get very busy but this still remains a pleasant and convenient spot to kick off your shoes, soak up in the sun and swim in the sea.

海滩靠近市区意味着这里很热闹，同时这里仍然是一个舒适的地方，可以光着脚丫做日光浴、在海里游泳。

5. There are numerous small restaurants and bars serving up tasty snacks and drinks.

有许多小餐馆和酒吧供应美味的小吃和饮料。

Chapter 8   Yalong Bay Tropical Paradise Forest Park

Yalong Bay Tropical Paradise Forest Park is located in the Yalong Bay National Resort in Sanya. The park, occupying an area of 15 square kilometers, is not only the first forest park in Sanya developed according to the specifications for National Forest Park of China, but also the first forest park for coastal mountain ecological tourism and resort.

There are two vegetation types in the park: tropical evergreen rainforest and tropical semi-deciduous forest. Counting on the great diversity of the biology, geography, astronomical phenomena and cultural resources, the park was constructed into a natural and ecological style. Multiple recreation activities are viable there such as mountain adventure, outward bound training, leisure, health resort, science education as well as folk culture experience. No wonder the Tropical Paradise is the nearest oxygen bar of natural forest to city.

Yalong Bay Tropical Paradise Forest Park has quite a few varieties of orchids. But there are a lot of stairs during the walk through the park, so be prepared for some exercise.

There is also an amazing rope bridge across a valley that gives a bird's-eye view of the landscape, but if you fear heights, it may not be fit for you. There is a cable ride about 0.6 kilometers on each of two segments down a long hillside that was a real blast.

You may choose to buy the photo taken by the staff as you are about to "land".

Once you are in the park, the great bus system will allow you to see even more of the park. Some of the roads were scary tough. The views are amazing and the forest is gorgeous.

On the hike up, you may see the countless butterflies and enjoy the natural beauty of the place. Once you arrive at the main peak and climb up the small pagoda at the top you will be treated to spectacular views spanning 360 degrees and covering Haitang Bay, Yalong Bay, Dadonghai, Sanya Bay, and Sanya City. You can also enjoy dinner at any restaurant there, and though it's a little bit pricey, the food is excellent and the views are unbeatable.

Bird Nest Resort is nestled here too. Leaning towards the hill and facing the sea, the Bird Nest Resort, built above the Yalong Bay with an uncommon construction method, is a perfect combination of mountain and luxury. The unique tropical style RUSTIC LUXURY HOTEL, which has a luxury content inside its simple appearance, possesses 142 sets of single-family homes and guestrooms managed by a professional mountain resort company. Constructed above the forest and surrounded by the cloud the Bird Nest Resort offers you a private space where you can overlook the sea joining the sky, enjoy the sunrise and sunset, listen to the singing birds outside the window in the morning and admire the brilliant light of the five-star hotel below.

Bird Nest Resort has 4. 2 square kilometers' plant landscape, 3 square kilometers' rock landscape and 0. 3 square kilometers' resort landscape. Greening area accounts for more than 85 percent. The average green area for each tourist is about 1. 5 square kilometers. At the top of the mountain, there are many facilities such as Liuyunxuan

Chinese Restaurant, Feilongling Western Restaurant, Haikuotiankong Tai Restaurant, Yalongge Multifunctional Restaurant, Mountain SPA Center and New Concept Outdoor Tents. Bird Nest Resort is your best option for rustic luxury holidays, romantic wedding, top end meeting, group activities as well as outdoor activities.

Grand Buddha Stone Panoramic Glass Skywalk is located at the top of the Tropical Paradise Forest Park. The highest point is 450 meters above sea level. The glass skywalk is built around the world's largest natural Buddha Maitreya stone. It is 400 meters long and 10 meters wide. It consists of 130 tons of super white imported glued glass, including aerial platform, colorful ladder, rainbow watchtower, rainbow road and so on. Walking on the glass skywalk, tourists can enjoy the blue sky and have a bird's-eye view of the rain forest valley more than 100 meters deep.

Notes:

1. The park, occupying an area of 15 square kilometers, is not only the first forest park in Sanya developed according to the specifications for National Forest Park of China, but also the first forest park for coastal mountain ecological tourism and resort.

公园占地面积15平方公里，是按照国家森林公园规范要求开发建设的三亚市第一个森林公园，也是第一座滨海山地生态观光兼生态度假型森林公园。

2. Multiple recreation activities are viable there such as mountain adventure, outward bound training, leisure, health resort, science education as well as folk culture experience.

园区有多种娱乐活动，如山地探险、拓展训练、休闲、疗养、科普教育、民俗文化体验等。

3. There is also an amazing rope bridge across a valley that gives a bird's-eye view of the landscape, but if you fear heights, it may not be fit for you.

　　峡谷上有一座很棒的索桥，可以俯瞰整个峡谷，但如果您恐高，那就不合适了。

　　4. Leaning towards the hill and facing the sea, the Bird Nest Resort, built above the Yalong Bay with an uncommon construction method, is a perfect combination of mountain and luxury.

　　亚龙湾的鸟巢度假区坐落在半山腰，面朝大海，建筑奇特，将自然山景与豪华设施完美结合。

　　5. Bird Nest Resort is your best option for rustic luxury holidays, romantic wedding, top end meeting, group activities as well as outdoor activities.

　　鸟巢度假区是乡村豪华假日、浪漫婚礼、高端会议、团体活动以及户外活动的最佳选择。

Part IV   Sanya (2)

This part will focus on...

· Nanshan Cultural Park;

· Luhuitou Park;

· Sanya Romance Park;

· Sanya Wax Work Museum;

· Seafood Night Markets;

· Eryue' er Festival;

· Sanyuesan Festival;

· Dragon Boat Festival.

Chapter 1   Nanshan Cultural Park

Sanya Nanshan Buddhism Cultural Tourism Zone is one of the largest cultural tourist attractions of its kind in China. It's located just 40 kilometers west of Sanya along the Hainan West Expressway. Countless visitors flock to the area, drawn by the beauty of Nanshan Mountain, making it a principal eco-tourism zone. Visitors are also attracted to the area because of the profound Buddhist influence on the surrounding culture. The zone features three theme parks: Buddhism Culture Park, Blessing and Longevity Park, and Hainan Custom Culture Park.

Buddhism Culture Park

Buddhism Culture Park was developed to bring the Buddhist culture to the masses and help them understand its profound philosophy. Highlights included the Nanshan Temple, the statue of the South China Sea Guanyin Bodhisattva, the China Buddhism

Culture Institute and the Guanyin Park. Visitors are awed by the giant sea-side statue of Guanyin which stands 108 meters high. A second statue of Guanyin, located nearby, stands 3.8 meters high and was constructed out of gold, diamonds and jade, along with other precious stones. It is said that its craftsmen used over 100 kilograms of gold to make this statue.

Blessing and Longevity Park embodies the essence of Chinese culture, conveying an atmosphere of peace and fortune.

Hainan Custom Culture Park is filled with the characteristics of Hainan Province. It takes advantage of its picturesque location to showcase tropical scenery and the customs of Li and Miao ethnic minorities.

Nanshan has been considered to be an auspicious and blessing land in Brahma. According to the record from Buddhism scriptures, the Guanyin Buddha vowed twelve oaths to save all living beings. To dwell at South Sea permanently is the second oath of the twelve. Master Jianzhen, the renowned monk in the Tang Dynasty, tried in vain five times to sail eastward to Japan for preach of Buddha's teaching. On his fifth sail to Japan, he was drifted to Nanshan. While staying in Nanshan for one year and a half, he set up a temple and did missionary work, and then, finally succeeded in his sixth voyage to Japan. The Japanese travel monk named Konghai also landed Nanshan on his way to learn Buddhism in the Tang Dynasty. The well-known saying "Good fortune as vast as East Sea, long life as great as Nanshan Mountain" shows further the Nanshan's origin of relations between Chinese traditional culture of auspiciousness and longevity.

Nanshan Buddhism Cultural Tourism Zone is a rare extra large-scale eco-cultural tourism zone with an area of 50 square kilometers including sea area of more than 10 square kilometers. With its harmony and beauty, Nanshan is now a tourist destination attracting more and more tourists coming from all over the world. It is here that people can enjoy themselves not only in the great tropical ecological environment with sunshine, sea, sand, blossom and greenery but also can feel with heart deep within the real beauty of peace and harmony of Buddhism culture and terse the joyfulness of returning to the nature.

Notes:

1. Visitors are awed by the giant sea-side statue of Guanyin which stands 108 meters high.

108 米高的巨型南海观音像令游客们叹为观止。

2. A second statue of Guanyin, located nearby, stands 3.8 meters high and was constructed out of gold, diamonds and jade, along with other precious stones.

附近的第二尊观音雕像高 3.8 米，用黄金、钻石和玉石等制成。

3. According to the record from Buddhism scriptures, the Guanyin Buddha vowed twelve oaths to save all living beings. To dwell at South Sea permanently is the second oath of the twelve.

根据佛教经典记载，观音菩萨普度众生有十二心愿，其第二心愿就是愿长居南海。

4. While staying in Nanshan for one year and a half, he set up a temple and did missionary work, and then, finally succeeded in his sixth voyage to Japan.

他在南山居住一年半之久并建造佛寺，传法布道，随后第六次东渡日本终获成功。

5. The well-known saying "Good fortune as vast as East Sea, long life as great as Nanshan Mountain" shows further the Nanshan's origin of relations between Chinese traditional culture of auspiciousness and longevity.

中国传扬千古的名句"福如东海，寿比南山"则更道出了南山与福寿文化的悠久渊源。

Chapter 2　Luhuitou Park

Luhuitou Park is situated on the hill near the seashore, 3 kilometers away from the Sanya in the south. Luhuitou Hill, at an altitude of about 280 meters, is the main peak of Luhuitou Peninsula. It's a pleasant place to appreciate the sunrise and sunset, and overlook the downtown area of Sanya. The name Luhuitou—a deer turning its head back—has been derived from a moving love story.

Long time ago, a tyrant emperor wanted a pair of velvet, so he forced a Li youngster named Ahei to hunt for deer on the mountainous area. On one occasion, while Ahei was hunting, he saw a beautiful spotted deer chased by a panther. He shot the panther to death with his arrow and run after the deer for nine days and nine nights. After passing ninety-nine hills, they arrived at the Coral Cliff of Sanya. The deer found no way to go except jumping into the sea while the hunter were bending his bow and got ready to shoot. Suddenly it turned its head back and changed into a beautiful girl walking toward him. Then, the hunter and the girl fell in love and married each other.

In the end, the fairy girl collected her brothers to defeat the tyrant and settled down on the cliff. After several generations' hard work, they finally built the Coral Cliff into a beautiful farm. From then on, the romantic hill has been called Luhuitou.

At present, a charming park had been built on the top of the Luhuitou and a huge sculpture with a length of 9 meters, a width of 4.9 meters and a height of 12 meters was set there based on the moving legend. So Sanya is also called "Deer City".

Starting from the foot of the hill, you can see various kinds of halobios, including starfish, crabs, sea cucumbers, actiniae and jellyfish. Up along the hill, a kind of red flower called Triangle Plum comes into view. It's the City Flower of Sanya. Halfway up the hill, a tuft of Triangle Plum, descending like a waterfall, is a really amazing sight. Not far from the flower and at the foot of an old tree stands a tablet inscribed with the red Chinese characters "Hai Shi Shan Meng" (a solemn pledge of love). On the branches of the old tree are hanging many ribbons indicating the permanent love of prayers. Walking along, you will see a pavilion called "Shanmeng" (unalterable love) Pavilion containing the Shanmeng Tablet, which corresponds to the four characters mentioned before. At the top of the hill towers a twelve-meter (39 feet) high granite statue. The statue is really unique in its design: consisting of a deer looking back, flanked by the young Li hunter and the beautiful fairy girl, which is a visual reminder of the memorable legend.

Luhuitou Peninsula is not only a romantic peninsula, but also a lush, natural environment covered with deciduous trees and plants. It is the ideal place to spend a winter holiday in China.

Notes:

1. Luhuitou Park is situated on the hill near the seashore, 3 kilometers away from the Sanya in the south.

鹿回头山顶公园坐落在海滨附近的山上，距离三亚市南部 3 公里。

2. It's a pleasant place to appreciate the sunrise and sunset, and overlook the

downtown area of Sanya.

这是欣赏日出日落、俯瞰三亚市区的好地方。

3. The name Luhuitou—a deer turning its head back—has been derived from a moving love story.

Luhuitou 意指鹿回头，源自一个动人的爱情故事。

4. At present, a charming park had been built on the top of the Luhuitou and a huge sculpture with a length of 9 meters, a width of 4.9 meters and a height of 12 meters was set there based on the moving legend.

如今，鹿回头山顶已建设成一座美丽的山顶公园，并根据美丽的传说在山上雕塑了一座高 12 米，长 9 米，宽 4.9 米的巨石雕像。

5. The statue is really unique in its design: consisting of a deer looking back, flanked by the young Li hunter and the beautiful fairy girl, which is a visual reminder of the memorable legend.

这座雕像的设计非常独特：一只鹿回头看，旁边站着黎族青年猎手和美丽的仙女，俨然是这个传奇故事的有形标志。

Chapter 3   Sanya Romance Park

Opened on 15th September 2013, the Sanya Romance Park, has become a must-go place on the itinerary of travelers to spend the night with friends and families in Sanya, thanks to its world-class entertainment which integrates modern technology, science-fiction, myths and legends and history and culture.

The Romance Park covers an area of 225 acres. With an investment of 1 billion yuan, it is made up of 10 theme zones, offering over 30 entertainment options.

Combining Sanya's traditional culture, Li and Miao culture and many other original folk customs, the theme park consists of a great many special areas and attractions, including Sanya Qianguqing Grand Theater, Yazhou Ancient City Cultural Theme Park, Elephant Valley, the Li and Miao Village Cultural Experience Area, Valentine's Valley, Children Playground, Banyan Bar, Triangle Plum Seafood Stall, South China Sea Goddness Cultural Square, and many more.

The scenic spot is only a 15-minute drive from Downtown Sanya and Yalong Bay. Here is one highlight to enjoy the theme park at night.

Sanya Qianguqing Grand Theater

The Legend of Romance is an indoor and panorama large-scale performance. It is based on Sanya history and mythology which is mixed by singing, dancing and acrobatics together. The performance will give you a pleasant and impressed feeling and can be compared beauty with the "Red Grindery" in Paris and "O Show" in Las Vegas. It is a must for the tourists coming to Sanya.

"The Legend of Romance" performance tells the history of Sanya from ancient to modern times through acrobatics, dance, and music. The one-hour shows featuring Sanya culture are performed at the theater daily, where can seat 4,700 people. The show has become the reputed program of the theme park and representative show in Sanya.

Notes:

1. Opened on 15th September 2013, the Sanya Romance Park, has become a must-go place on the itinerary of travelers to spend the night with friends and families in Sanya, thanks to its world-class entertainment which integrates modern technology, science-fiction, myths and legends and history and culture.

三亚千古情自 2013 年 9 月 15 日开业，已经成为游客们在三亚与朋友和家人夜游的一个去处。这得益于它的国际级表演，融合了现代科技、科幻小说、神话传说和历史文化。

2. The Romance Park covers an area of 225 acres. With an investment of 1 billion yuan, it is made up of 10 theme zones, offering over 30 entertainment options.

三亚千古情占地 225 英亩，投资 10 亿元，由 10 个主题区组成，提供超过 30 个娱乐选项。

3. It is based on Sanya history and mythology which is mixed by singing, dancing and acrobatics together.

它是以三亚历史和神话为基础，融歌唱、舞蹈、杂技于一体。

4. The one-hour shows featuring Sanya culture are performed at the theater daily,

where can seat 4,700 people.

长达一个小时的三亚文化特色演出每天都在可容纳4 700人的剧院上演。

5. The show has become the reputed program of the theme park and representative show in Sanya.

该演出已成为三亚主题公园知名的、具有代表性的节目。

Chapter 4   Sanya Wax Work Museum

Sanya Wax Work Museum is located in the famous scenic spot area of Dadonghai. It is the first one of its kind in Sanya open to tourists. The wax works are all designed, created and made by Chinese artists with the exhibition hall of 1,500 square meters. The wax works figures are consisting of historical figures, movie stars, sports stars, political figures, business tycoons, and so on. It brings the visitors a visual and auditory feast, and allows visitors to experience the fun of going through the ancient, current and future time. The interesting and magnificent characters entertain children and adults at the same time. The modern technology is fully used in the design and the beautifully decorated space will leave you a good memory for your Sanya trip.

Notes:

1. Sanya Wax Work Museum is located in the famous scenic spot area of Dadonghai.

三亚蜡像馆位于著名的大东海风景名胜区。

2. The wax works are all designed, created and made by Chinese artists with the exhibition hall of 1,500 square meters.

这座蜡像馆全部由中国艺术家设计、创作和制作，展厅面积 1 500 平方米。

3. The wax works figures are consisting of historical figures, movie stars, sports stars, political figures, business tycoons, and so on.

蜡像包括一些历史人物、电影明星、体育明星、政治人物、商业大亨等。

Chapter 5   Seafood Night Markets

Sanya, China's southernmost city, perched on the coast of tropical Hainan Island, is a seafood lover's dream destination. Its proximity to the ocean and large fishing fleet keep the city teeming with some of the freshest seafood.

There are plenty of restaurants, but a visit to one of the city's markets is the best way to sample the latest catch. Chunyuan Seafood Square at Tianya Street is popular with locals.

Another popular local spot is No. 1 Market at Xinjian Street and Xinmin Street. These busy markets sell an amazing variety of seafood—hele crabs, lobster, scallops, shellfish, amberjack, sea bream, squirrel fish, snapper, carol fish, grouper and so on.

Grab your purchase and take it to one of the nearby restaurants or open air food courts who will cook it up for a small fee. You can order them to steam or fry with light or spicy flavor. In this way, you can enjoy the delicious seafood at a less pricey price.

Notes：

1．Chunyuan Seafood Square at Tianya Street is popular with locals.

位于天涯街的春园海鲜广场受当地人喜欢。

2．Another popular local spot is No. 1 Market at Xinjian Street and Xinmin Street.

另一个受欢迎的地方是位于新建街和新民街的第一市场。

3．These busy markets sell an amazing variety of seafood—hele crabs, lobster, scallops, shellfish, amberjack, sea bream, squirrel fish, snapper, carol fish, grouper and so on.

这个热闹的市场销售各种令人惊艳的海鲜——和乐蟹、龙虾、扇贝、贝类、琥珀鱼、海鲤、松鼠鱼、鲷鱼、卡罗鱼和石斑鱼等。

4．Grab your purchase and take it to one of the nearby restaurants or open air food courts who will cook it up for a small fee.

带上您买的海鲜到附近的某家餐馆或者露天美食广场，他们会收取低额的加工费帮您烹饪。

5．You can order them to steam or fry with light or spicy flavor.

您可以下单：清蒸或辣炒。

Chapter 6　Eryue' er Festival

Eryue' er Festival or Dragons-raise-heads Festival is a traditional Chinese festival for many ethnic groups, including Han, Li, Miao, Zhuang, Man, Dong and other smaller ethnic groups. It falls on February 2nd of the Chinese lunar calendar. The earliest record about this festival could be gone back to the Tang Dynasty (618 – 907 AD). Bai Juyi, a great poet of the Tang Dynasty wrote a poem to relive the celebration of this festival, "On Eryue' er, the first rounds of spring rain falls gently on the tender grass and vegetable; along the X-shaped ferry, lightly-dressed young people walk in single file with their horses. "

People have a spring out to appreciate the beauty of the season on this festival. They also have some ceremony activities such as offering vegetables and fruits as a symbol of fortune to friends and relatives. From the Ming Dynasty (1368 – 1644 AD), there were more dragon-related activities on this festival. And this festival is also called Dragons-raise-heads Festival. In Chinese mythology, the great dragons are in charge of rain and wind, which are of great importance to agriculture. Therefore, people celebrate this festival to pray for good climate and harvests.

Hainan Island has been the home of dragons in Chinese Mythology long ago. Therefore, the worship to dragons is extremely popular and important here. Every coastal village has a temple of the great dragons for people to worship. The fishermen also worship the great dragons and celebrate the Eryue' er Festival for good luck of fishing activities and fishing journey on the sea.

From 2005, on every Eryue' er Festival, there is a government organized grand ceremony to worship the great Dragons and the sea on the scenic spot of Dongtian Park in Taoism Ways. Nowadays, in addition to the traditional praying for harvest and fortune, local people introduced new elements into activities, such as environmental-protection campaigns. They believe that by celebrating the Dragons-raise-heads Festival, China will be more and more prosperous and Chinese people, who believe that they are the offspring of the great dragons, will enjoy happier life and well-to-do time.

Notes:

1. Eryue' er Festival or Dragons-raise-heads Festival is a traditional Chinese festival for many ethnic groups, including Han, Li, Miao, Zhuang, Man, Dong and other smaller ethnic groups.

二月二或龙抬头节是中国多个民族的传统节日，包括汉、黎、苗、壮、满、侗和其他的少数民族。

2. In Chinese mythology, the great dragons are in charge of rain and wind, which are of great importance to agriculture.

在中国神话中，海龙王掌管着对农业至关重要的雨和风。

3. Therefore, people celebrate this festival to pray for good climate and harvests.

因此，人们庆祝这个节日是为了祈求好气候和丰收。

4. The fishermen also worship the great dragons and celebrate the Eryue' er Festival for good luck of fishing activities and fishing journey on the sea.

渔民也在二月二祭祀龙王，为捕鱼活动和捕鱼之旅举办祈福庆典。

5. Nowadays, in addition to the traditional praying for harvest and fortune, local people introduced new elements into activities, such as environmental-protection campaigns.

如今，除了传统的丰收和财富祈求仪式之外，当地人也在这个节日里引入了新的元素，例如环保活动。

Chapter 7　Sanyuesan Festival

Sanyuesan Festival falls on March 3rd in Chinese lunar calendar, and it has long been an important traditional festival in China. It is observed and celebrated by many Chinese ethnic groups, including the local Li people, as the festival for lovers to express their love for each other. In a sense, it is the Valentine's Day for some ethnic groups.

It is said that March 3rd in Chinese lunar calendar is the birthday of Emperor Yellow, who has been considered in Chinese mythology to be the ancestor of all Chinese people, including all the ethnic groups in China. Various ethnic groups celebrate this festival in their own specific ways, usually involving lovers to express their love by means of dancing, singing, chatting softly, or mutual exchange of love letters or gifts. Du Fu, a great Chinese poet of the Tang Dynasty relived the festival in one of his poems. The first line is as followed, "Folks enjoy the fine weather of the approaching spring on Sanyuesan, appreciating groups of stunning beauties of the royal family strolling on the riverside of Chang' an. "

The local Li ethnic groups observe Sanyuesan Festival as their biggest festival. It is a festival for praying for the harvest of crops and successful hunting. However, the most important content and all the major celebrating activities are related to love and wedding. Therefore, Sanyuesan is also called Day of Love by Li people.

From ancient time, in every Sanyuesan Festival, Li people dress their best and most formal ethnic clothes, and carry bottles of homemade rice wine and delicious rice in bamboo containers to gather together for this carnival, usually under a palm tree or on a big open area in a rubber plantation. They play unique music instruments, dance and sing folk songs with their beloved ones, including family members, old and new friends.

In addition, young lads go to fish in streams and young girls cook and make some Li-style barbecue, while other people lay out snacks and pray in front of a statue of Guanyin Goddess for harvest and good luck. After the praying ceremony, young people will have some sport entertainments such as arrow shooting, coconut tree climbing, playing on the swings to have fun together. When it turns dark, they dance around bonfire in various fabulous, energetic, and interactive ways. Young girls wear glittering jewelry and ornaments in the evening while young men carry colorful umbrellas and dance around them to flirt and express love. If a girl and a boy like each other, they will go to a quieter corner in the wood and exchange the love gift they prepared in advance. In most cases, boys give a jewelry item and girls give a piece of Li brocade as the presents. And then they will talk softly and gently for hours till the dawn comes.

Sanyuesan Festival is definitely a perfect occasion for finding love.

Notes:

1. It is said that March 3rd in Chinese lunar calendar is the birthday of Emperor Yellow, who has been considered in Chinese mythology to be the ancestor of all Chinese people, including all the ethnic groups in China.

据说，农历三月初三是黄帝的生日，他在中国神话中被认为是中国各民族的祖先。

2. Various ethnic groups celebrate this festival in their own specific ways, usually involving lovers to express their love by means of dancing, singing, chatting softly, or mutual exchange of love letters or gifts.

各民族以自己的方式庆祝节日，通常是有情人通过跳舞、唱歌、聊天、互致情书或礼物来表达爱意。

3. However, the most important content and all the major celebrating activities are related to love and wedding.

然而，最重要的内容和主要的庆祝活动都与爱情和婚礼有关。

4. From ancient time, in every Sanyuesan Festival, Li people dress their best and most formal ethnic clothes, and carry bottles of homemade rice wine and delicious rice in bamboo containers to gather together for this carnival, usually under a palm tree or on a big open area in a rubber plantation.

自古以来，每到"三月三"，黎族人会穿上他们最好的、最正式的民族服装，携带自制的米酒、竹筒饭齐聚一堂欢庆节日，通常是在棕榈树下或橡胶园的大片空地上。

5. If a girl and a boy like each other, they will go to a quieter corner in the wood and exchange the love gift they prepared in advance.

如果一个女孩和一个男孩互相喜欢对方，他们会去树林里一个安静的角落，交换他们预先准备好的爱情信物。

Chapter 8   Dragon Boat Festival

Dragon Boat Festival falls on May 5th of Chinese lunar calendar, which was originated from ancient China. Today the best known origin of the festival is to honor Qu Yuan, a poet and statesman of the Chu Kingdom during the Warring States Period in 278 BC. He was a descendant of the Chu royal family and served as a high-rank official. However, when the king decided to ally with the increasingly powerful State of Qin, Qu was banished for opposing the alliance. During his exile, Qu Yuan wrote a great deal of poetry which have been read until now. Twenty-eight years later, Qin conquered the Chu capital. In despair, Qu Yuan committed suicide by drowning himself in the Miluo River on May 5th of Chinese lunar calendar.

It is said that the local people rushed to save him by rowing boat as quickly as possible, which is believed to be the origin of dragon boat racing. Then the folks threw food into the river to feed the fish so that they would not bite Qu Yuan's body, which has passed on to Chinese people eating Zongzi on this festival.

On every Dragon Boat Festival, dragon boat contest is a popular festival activity attracting thousands of people. Usually it is carried out on the Sanya River, giving great fun to the local people as well as tourists of Sanya. In the sound of drums, numerous spectators would flock to the port or flank the river banks to cheer for their favorable teams. The contestants, for their own honor and the entertainment of the folks, would strive to reach the finish line by braving the waves.

Notes:

1. Today the best known origin of the festival is to honor Qu Yuan, a poet and statesman of the Chu Kingdom during the Warring States Period in 278 BC.

如今，这个节日流传最广的起源就是纪念公元前 278 年战国时期楚国诗人、政治家屈原。

2. In despair, Qu Yuan committed suicide by drowning himself in the Miluo River on May 5th of Chinese lunar calendar.

绝望中，屈原于农历五月初五在汨罗河投河自尽。

3. It is said that the local people rushed to save him by rowing boat as quickly as possible, which is believed to be the origin of dragon boat racing.

当地人赶紧划船来救他，据说这就是赛龙舟的起源。

4. On every Dragon Boat Festival, dragon boat contest is a popular festival activity attracting thousands of people.

每年的端午节，赛龙舟这一庆典活动吸引了成千上万的人。

5. Usually it is carried out on the Sanya River, giving great fun to the local people as well as tourists of Sanya.

它通常是在三亚河上进行，给三亚市民和游客们带来许多欢乐。

Part V   Eastern Part of Hainan

This part will focus on…

- introduction to eastern part of Hainan;
- Ding' an;
- Wenchang;
- Qionghai;
- Wanning;
- Lingshui.

Chapter 1　Introduction to Eastern Part of Hainan

Eastern part of Hainan consists of cities or counties of Ding' an, Wenchang, Qionghai, Wanning, Lingshui, where National Highway No. 223 and Eastern Highway run through. It has abundant sunshine and rainwater. It is the earliest area for Hainan' s economic and tourist development, equipped with the most perfect facilities and the richest culture. Generally, most tours around the island will choose this route.

With the most convenient transport, the scenic spots have been flourishing: Wenchang is famous for its coconut culture, where is teeming with coconut trees; Qionghai is well known for Bo' ao Forum for Asia and Wanquan River; Xinglong Tropical Botanical Garden in Wanning features in exotic Southeast Asia; Lingshui is home to Macaque Nature Reserve in China—Nanwan Monkey Island.

The eastern tour route is a tour of delicacy, for most of the famous food originated from these places, where seafood is abundant. For example, Dongjiao in Wenchang and Bo' ao in Qionghai are famous seafood producing areas. The seafood courts here are famous for their freshest flavor and fair prices. Tourists can eat delicious seafood such as abalone, crab, mussel, lobster, sea urchin. To look for the best taste, it is necessary to eat along the eastern part of Hainan, either in luxury restaurants or sidewalk snack booths. In addition, Wanning Dazhou Island is home to the best bird' s nests. In Xinglong, you can also have a taste of authentic Indonesian food.

Scores of natural hot springs lie in the eastern part of Hainan, as well. Guantang Hot Spring in Qionghai and Xinglong Hot Spring in Wanning are known as unique in

Hainan and rare in the world.

At present, the eastern tourism industry has been thriving and supporting facilities have been greatly improved. In the future, it will continue to be a powerful force for tourism.

Notes:

1. It is the earliest area for Hainan's economic and tourism development, equipped with the most perfect facilities and the richest culture.

这是海南经济与旅游开发最早、设施最完善、文化传统最深厚的地区。

2. With the most convenient transport, the scenic spots have been flourishing: Wenchang is famous for its coconut culture, where is teeming with coconut trees; Qionghai is well known for Bo'ao Forum for Asia and Wanquan River; Xinglong Tropical Botanical Garden in Wanning features in exotic Southeast Asia; Lingshui is home to Macaque Nature Reserve in China——Nanwan Monkey Island.

由于交通最为便捷，这些景区业已蓬勃发展：文昌以椰文化著称，那儿有最为繁茂的椰林；琼海以博鳌亚洲论坛及万泉河出名；万宁兴隆热带植物园尽显东南亚风情；陵水拥有岛屿型猕猴自然保护区——南湾猴岛。

3. The eastern tour route is a tour of delicacy, for most of the famous food originated from these places, where seafood is abundant.

东线之旅可谓美食之旅，因为大部分的著名美食的发源地几乎都在东线，这里盛产海鲜。

4. To look for the best taste, it is necessary to eat along the eastern part of Hainan, either in luxury restaurants or sidewalk snack booths.

要品尝正宗原味还非得在东线一带吃不可，不管是高档酒楼还是大排档都好吃。

5. Guantang Hot Spring in Qionghai and Xinglong Hot Spring in Wanning are known as unique in Hainan and rare in the world.

琼海官塘温泉和万宁兴隆温泉号称海南罕见，世界少有。

Chapter 2   Ding' an

Ding' an is located in the northeast of Hainan, covering an area of 1,189 square kilometers. The seat of government in Ding' an is only 33 kilometers away from Haikou. It is about 50 minutes drive from Haikou Meilan International Airport, or 2 hours from Sanya Phoenix International Airport.

Take a short trip around Ding' an and you will find yourself surrounded by the honest custom of the local people and pleasant living environment. Ding' an is well known as the "Food Paradise" "Tropical Cold Spring of Asia" "Longevity Hometown of China" and "Kingdom of Tropical Birds".

If you come to Ding'an, you can visit the following attractions:

Wenbi Peak

Wenbi Peak, also called Wenhao Peak, is located in the middle part of Ding' an. It is rising abruptly out of the ground, elegant and beautiful. Wenbi Peak is regarded as one of the Eight Views of Ding' an. On October 29th, 2012, Wenbi Peak was officially listed as a national 4A-level Scenic Spot in Hainan. With its increasing Taoist cultural influence, the solemnness and mystery of scenic areas have attracted numerous tourists who search for peace of mind and spiritual satisfaction.

There is an old story about the Wenbi Peak. Long ago, one immortal shouldered two loads of soil to the Peach Garden of the Goddess. When he passed Ding' an, he was attracted by the picturesque scenery, and laid down to have a rest. He was drinking while appreciating the scene. Unconsciously, he was drunk and fell into sleep. After a long time of sleeping, the immortal changed into stone, and the two loads changed into mountains, one of which is the Wenbi Peak.

On Wenbi Peak, there are many relics of the immortal, namely, Immortal Cave, Immortal Footprint, Immortal Palm, Immortal Rock and Fairy Cave.

On the east and west side of the Wenbi Peak, the mountains are composed of igneous rocks, with a history of one million years. However, the hydrogenic rocks at top of the Wenbi Peak has a history of hundreds of million years, which is rare in geography.

Jiuwentang Cold Spring

Jiuwentang Cold Spring is a truly rare natural spring with temperatures of 23℃ to 25℃. This kind of unique spring is only found elsewhere in Italy and Taiwan, China. The water of the cold spring is odorless, clear and drinkable and contains sodium bicarbonate.

The spring is located at Jiuwentang Village, Longmen Town. The water is freezing cold on the first five minutes of dipping, but the body quickly warms up. Since the bubbles keep popping up from the bottom, bathing in this spring water feels like bathing in sugar-free sodas.

It is a free public bathing area, and the cold spring will help urge your blood circulation to work regularly and thoroughly. If you are in Ding' an, don' t miss the chance to enjoy this amazing cold spring.

Nanli Lake

Nanli Lake Scenery Area is one of the famous artificial freshwater lakes among the first group of scenery areas at the provincial level. You can go boating on the lake, while enjoying a beautiful picture of trees and water.

As a scenic site, Nanli Lake offers accommodation, catering and entertainment.

More important is that the facilities here are ample, including a golf course, sumptuous hotels, restaurants, villas, and some facilities of water entertainment.

Hainan Tropical Bird Park

Hainan Tropical Bird Park is located at the Taling development zone in Ding' an. The park boasts three hundred types of tropical birds, including many unique Hainan birds.

Visitors to the park can also enjoy a 32-meter-long and 3.8-meter-high wall with relief sculptures of nine phoenixes, a rainforest for birds, a bird park and a parrot square.

Qiongju Opera

Ding' an has always been known as the hometown of Qiongju Opera. Qiongju Opera, also known as Qiongzhou Opera and Hainan Opera, is a local folk opera art. It is one of the branches of Southern Opera. It mainly uses Hainan dialect as the language of opera. Therefore, the popular area is limited to Hainan Island and Guangdong Province. It is one of the local cultural symbols. On the seasons of celebration and festivals, each village collects money to invite Qiong Opera Troupe to perform at the village, which is very popular among local villagers. In June 2008, Qiongju Opera was approved by the State Council and listed in the second batch of national intangible cultural heritage.

Qiongju Opera has rich artistic heritage, and its traditional repertoire is divided into three parts: first, singing opera. Originating from Yiyang Opera, it mixes with Siping and Qingyang Opera, which belongs to the Qupai system, with well-developed roll singing. Some famous operas include *The Story of Huaiyin* and *The Story of Pipa*. Second, kungfu opera, such as *The Romance of the Three Kingdoms*, *Water Margin*, *General Yang* and *Creation of Gods*. Third, modern drama, featured in Chinese tunic suit and cheongsam, such as

National Salvation Movement, The Sacrifice of Qiujin.

The costumes used to be crown robes of the Han and Ming Dynasties. Official robes were all embroidered with velvet. The colors of costumes of scholars, village girls and robbers were limited in white, black, blue and red. Boots and shoes were all made of thin soles but soldiers and robbers wear grass shoes. After the founding of the People' s Republic of China, reforms have been made to design costumes according to the needs of scripts.

Since 1978, Haikou Qiong Theatre and theatre troupes in various cities and counties have gradually revived. Excellent traditional plays have been restaged, and theatre organizations have been restored successively. The young actors trained by Qiongju schools have gradually become the backbone of the new generation. Drama creation and research work has been carried out normally, and many popular scripts have been created.

In 1982, the provincial Qiong Opera Troupe of China visited Singapore and Thailand to perform and received good reviews. Since then, Guangdong Qiong Theatre, Hainan Youth Qiong Opera Troupe and Hainan Qiong Opera Troupe have visited Singapore, Thailand, Malaysia, Hong Kong and other countries and regions. Xinxinggang and Qiongliansheng Opera Troupes from Singapore also came to visit and perform successively. The artistic exchanges with Qiong Opera Troupes in Singapore, Malaysia, Thailand and Hong Kong have become increasingly frequent. At present, there are over 17 professional Qiong Opera Troupes or academies in Hainan Province, and nearly 100 amateur opera troupes in counties, towns and villages.

Vegetable-packed Rice

Vegetable-packed rice is a special snack for the locals in Ding' an, which has a history of over a hundred years. The local people like to eat it for it has special meaning, that is, "work together, and gather family wealth all in a piece". Packed rice is a kind of eating method that mixes meat,

vegetables and rice, wrapped in vegetable leaves and eaten in hands.

It takes a lot of efforts to make vegetable-packed rice. Firstly, let cooked rice become cool; secondly, prepare clean lettuce; thirdly, prepare other vegetables with strong flavor, and meat, such as garlic, celery, leek, onion, kidney beans, hot pepper, pickles, together with pork, chicken, sausage and so on. After the raw materials are ready, the vegetables and meat are fried first, then the garlic, shrimp and squid are fried and fried them dry in a pot, and finally the vegetables and meat are poured into the rice to mix well.

You don't have to worry about the image when you eat vegetable-packed rice. When you eat, you can also put your favorite sauces such as shrimp sauce, chili sauce or assorted sauce onto the lettuce. Please eat it while it's hot, and keep your mouth wide open to have a nice bite. You may feel a particular flavor although your hands are full of oil or rice or something. Nowadays, it is very popular among the people of Dingcheng and its neighboring villages in Ding'an.

Ding'an Zongzi

Ding'an Zongzi was served from the Ming Dynasty and it is one of the three famous brands in Hainan. In recent years, since Ding'an Cultural Festival was founded in the county, Ding'an Zongzi has been sold all over the country and overseas, and is highly praised and well-known. The raw materials are selenium-rich rice and selenium-rich black pork. Rice is prepared with salt, spices and other condiments. Streaky pork and salted duck eggs is the main ingredient. Carefully and skillfully, all is wrapped, and then cooked in a pot for about ten hours before they are ready. The production process is very exquisite and the flavor is nicer.

Notes:

1. With its increasing Taoist cultural influence, the solemnness and mystery of

scenic areas have attracted numerous tourists who search for peace of mind and spiritual satisfaction.

随着道教文化影响力的不断增强，这个庄严而又神秘的景区吸引了无数寻求心灵宁静和精神安慰的游客。

2. After a long time of sleeping, the immortal changed into stone, and the two loads changed into mountains, one of which is the Wenbi Peak.

睡了很长时间后，神仙变成石头，两堆土变成了山脉，其中一座就是文笔峰。

3. It is a free public bathing area, and the cold spring will help urge your blood circulation to work regularly and thoroughly.

这是一个免费的公共洗浴区，冷泉有助于促进血液循环。

4. Nanli Lake Scenery Area is one of the famous artificial freshwater lakes among the first group of scenery areas at the provincial level.

南丽湖风景区是一个著名的人工淡水湖，是第一批省级风景区。

5. Originating from Yiyang Opera, it mixes with Siping and Qingyang Opera, which belongs to the Qupai system, with well-developed roll singing. Some famous operas include *The Story of Huaiyin* and *The Story of Pipa*.

它源于弋阳腔，杂以四平、青阳二腔，属曲牌体制，滚唱发达，著名剧目包括《槐荫记》《琵琶记》。

Chapter 3 Wenchang

Wenchang is 40 kilometers from Haikou's Meilan International Airport. Engulfed by the sea on three sides, Wenchang has many great bays and beaches. It has a coastline of 206. 07 kilometers, including 40 bays. Wenchang's total area is 2,488 square kilometers, taking up 7% of Hainan Island.

Wenchang is famous for its hometown of overseas Chinese, with a large number of talented people. It is the hometown of most overseas Hainanese migrants from Southeast Asia. The fabulous Song Family also came from Wenchang, and now Song Qingling's Former Residence is one of the scenic attractions. Wenchang dialect is considered to be the standard dialect of Hainan for media broadcasting and Hainan Opera. It is also known for a love of volleyball and abundant coconut trees.

If you come to visit Wenchang, please don't miss the following attractions:

The Wenchang Satellite Launch Center

Because of the position and low latitude of Wenchang, a new satellite launch center has been built there to launch satellites. Covering about 20 square kilometers, this center includes a rocket assembly plant, a command center and facilities such as a space research center and a theme park.

As the new launch center faces the sea to its south and east, large rockets can be easily shipped to the center and launch debris will plunge into the water. Moreover, the center is close to residential areas and Haikou, so it is expected to play an important role in boosting the local economy and tourism. Currently, it has become a popular science base that attracts thousands of students all over the Island yearly.

Wenchang Confucius Temple

The temple was first built during the 11th century, and had undergone repeated renovation and expansion since the Ming Dynasty. The temple is also one of the biggest and most impressive examples of ancient architectures in Hainan. It is strictly built according to the uniform structure of Confucius temples throughout China, strictly based on Chinese architectural principles of symmetry.

Entering the gate, the first thing you see is a life-sized statue of Confucius. Further back is a wooden hall, where the calligraphy of famous and powerful emperors is on display. In the middle of the hall, memorial tablets dedicated to Confucius and his twelve best disciples are well placed. In the two side rooms there are tributes including painting and calligraphic work by famous artists. Also there are replicas of 72 Confucian disciples' portraits (the originals are on display in the Confucius Temples in Shandong and Beijing). Every year, people hold activities to honor Confucius.

Tonggu Ridge Tourist Zone

Tonggu Ridge Tourist Zone is located in the northeast coast of Longlou Town, 40 kilometers away from Wencheng Town, capital of Wenchang. It covers an area of 84. 3 square kilometers, which includes land area of 44. 3 square kilometers, and sea area of 40 square kilometers. Its peak is 338 meters high, accompanied by 18 different sizes of mountains.

It is not only one of the ten major provincial tourist zones but also one of the first tourist projects in China. Integrating unique mountain, grotto and tropical rainforest, Tonggu Ridge Tourist Zone is proved to be an amazing tourist destination for vocation and sightseeing.

Dongjiao Coconut Plantation

Dongjiao Coconut Plantation is located on the seaside of Dongjiao Town. The lush coconut plantation forms an endless tree belt, like a natural green barrier on the coast.

Because of huge coconut plantations and the great yield of coconut, Wenchang is known as " Home to Coconut", accounting for more than 50% of the total in the province. In Dongjiao town, coconut palms can be seen in stretches and in varied shapes. The plantation is literally a forest with over 500,000 coconut trees including different varieties. There goes a saying that the yield of coconuts in Wenchang is responsible for half of that grown in Hainan and the best quality comes from Dongjiao Coconut Plantation.

With typical coconut and coastal scenery, the area lures many tourists with special coconut food and drinks, and a variety of seafood. Unique wooden cottages facing the sea are scattered in the woods. The furnishings inside are plain but in natural, antique style. The cottages are equipped with facilities of suite. Sitting under the roof, you can enjoy your tea contentedly or just look at the sea. The beach there is a good place for shooting the sunset.

Wenchang Chicken

Wenchang Chicken is one of Hainan' s four specialties, and may be the most well known of all. Not only popular in Hainan, it has also become a signature dish in Hong Kong and Southeast Asia, due to the nostalgia for their home of the Hainanese. The chickens are generally free-range chickens. Wenchang Chicken is normally boiled and then cut into pieces. It is then eaten by dipping the pieces in a mixture of spices including chopped ginger, garlic, salt, soy sauce, vinegar, and freshly squeezed citrus. The skin of Wenchang Chicken is typically yellow, with an oily appearance, and the inner meat and bones

appears a little bit red and raw-looking. This chicken tastes tender, delicious but not greasy.

Baoluo Rice Noodles

Baoluo Rice Noodles are made of rice noodles with various toppings, most commonly a thick meat gravy with thin strips of bamboo or delicious soup. Crowning the snack is pork and beef jerky, cooked until browned and tender, and peanuts, fried until crispy and golden. The name is from the most famous rice noodle in Baoluo Town of Wenchang, as the noodles thicker than "Hainan Rice Noodles", the northern people of Hainan also called it "thick rice noodles soup".

Jinshan Fried Sesame Balls

Fried sesame balls are commonly known as "treasure bags" in Hainan. These sesame balls are usually filled with shredded, sweetened coconut or nuts. Because of their auspicious symbol, people often send them as gifts on wedding occasions and eat them at festivals. Moreover, they have become local people's favorite breakfast or snacks for their tasty flavor.

Notes:

1. Covering about 20 square kilometers, this center includes a rocket assembly plant, a command center and facilities such as a space research center and a theme park.

发射中心占地约 20 平方公里，包括一个火箭装配厂、一个指挥中心和一个航天研究中心等设施，以及一个主题公园。

2. It is strictly built according to the uniform structure of Confucius temples throughout China, strictly based on Chinese architectural principles of symmetry.

它是严格根据中国孔子庙的建筑结构标准而打造，严格以中国建筑的对称性为基础设计原则。

3. Entering the gate, the first thing you see is a life-sized statue of Confucius.

走进大门，首先见到的是一尊真人大小的孔子雕像。

4. There goes a saying that the yield of coconuts in Wenchang is responsible for half of that grown in Hainan and the best quality comes from Dongjiao Coconut Plantation.

有句俗话说：文昌椰子半海南，东郊椰子最风光。

5. Crowning the snack is pork and beef jerky, cooked until browned and tender, and peanuts, fried until crispy and golden.

这道小吃的精华是外焦里嫩的猪肉干、牛肉干，和酥脆金黄的花生米。

Chapter 4 Qionghai

Qionghai is situated in the east part of Hainan Island, 86 kilometers from Haikou.

Qionghai has a long history with its own culture and abundant natural resources. People here are modest, hospitable, and open-minded. For a long time, Qionghai has been known to investors and tourists for a relaxing environment, good public security, balanced environment, and efficient administration.

Bo' ao, seat of the Bo' ao Forum for Asia, is located in Qionghai. The Bo' ao Forum for Asia is a non-profit organization that hosts high-level forums for leaders from government, business and academia in Asia and other continents to share their vision on the most pressing issues in this dynamic region and the whole world.

Qionghai is charming with the world-famous Wanqian River at its heart. The Qionghai tourist area is comprised of Bo' ao Watertown, Wanqian River, Bo' ao Jade Belt Beach, Baishi Ridge, and Guantang Hot Springs.

Bo' ao Watertown

Bo' ao Watertown is situated at a unique coast of Bo' ao Town, emerging at the meeting points of three famous rivers (Wanquan, Jiuqu, and Longgun), and characterized by rivers, lakes, sea, sandy beach, mountains, hot spring, etc.

In the past, Bo' ao was a small quiet village, where people made a living by fishing at sea. It is now famous thanks to the annual Asia Forum.

The outlet of the Wanquan River to the sea is also the confluence of the Longgun River and the Jiuqu River. Time and tide have created some magnificent sandbanks and islets. So far, this area is the best-preserved river exit to the sea in the world. The water, the beaches, the green forests on the seashore, the coconut palms swaying in sea breezes and the cooking smoke in nearby villages all contribute to making Bo' ao a natural miracle.

Jade Belt Beach

Located on the southern bank of the estuary of Wanquan River, Jade Belt Beach lies in east of Bo' ao Water-town and extends in a North-South direction, with only a narrow strip connected with land, just like a long "jade belt" that separates the Wanquan River from the South China Sea, forming a long and narrow natural beach. The widest distance is 300 – 500 meters, and the narrowest is only 10 meters wide.

In June, 1999, Jade Belt Beach was listed in Guinness World Records by the Guinness Shanghai headquarters for having "the narrowest sand peninsula to separate a river from the sea".

Wanquan River Tourism Zone

Wanquan River has been well conserved and named as the mother river in Hainan.

The whole length of Wanquan River is 163 kilometers, originated from Wuzhi Mountain. Along the upper reaches are marvelous peaks, flourishing coconut trees along the river. Tourists are fascinated by the charming water scenery. Along the lower reaches are densely covered by ports and people can enjoy

themselves so much by the scenes which are full of pastoral characteristics.

To protect eco-environment, scenery designers have showed great respect to the nature and finally a series of tourist attractions containing river thrilling drift, valley exploration, and night drift emerged.

It takes more than 2 hours to go through the entire drift. Along the course, you gain opportunity to experience excitement while journeying along the river to feast your eyes with natural beauty on either bank.

Valley exploration constitutes of a number of thrilling programs such as rowing up against rapid current, going through the rainforest, and jumping off the cliff, which is sure a challenge to conquer fear.

Tourists will find it incredible to experience this exciting drift while enjoying the beautiful scenery along the journey.

The Red Detachment of Women

The Red Detachment of Women is well-known nationwide thanks to the grand ballet *The Red Detachment of Women*. At Jiaji Town, a memorial garden has been built to commemorate the first female army force in Hainan Province. A sculpture of a female soldier stands prominently in the garden.

The statue is made of granite, with 6.8 meters high from the top to the base. The female soldier stands upright, wearing the red army uniform, with a bamboo hat at her back, and a rifle on her shoulder. She wears grass shoes on her feet, with the bandage tied around her shanks. It shows us a lively woman soldier, looking very vigorous and impressive.

In the history of Chinese revolution, the Red Detachment of Women was the first female army force in Hainan. During the civil war, they coordinated with the main force of the red army, fought bravely and made great contributions not only to the revolutionary cause of Hainan Island but also to the revolutionary cause of the whole nation.

Whenever talking about the Red Detachment of Women, the local people always feel proud of them. It is a good example to show that women are as important as men. Now the memorial garden has become an patriotic education base, and a number of students and communist party members come here to show their respect yearly.

Baishi Ridge

Baishi Ridge is located by the Wanquan River, 12 kilometers to the southwest of Qionghai. It's attractive and popular because of the wonderful hills, spectacular rocks and fascinating caves. At the top of Baishi Ridge stands a gigantic egg-shaped rock in white, so the attraction of Baishi Ridge is named after this rock. This gigantic rock weights thousands of tons. Half of the rock is sandwiched by the other two rocks while another half is hanging in the air. By the gigantic rock there is an interesting cave. When a strong wind occurs and runs through it, some nice whistling is produced, making nice music out of the wind. From the foot of the hill to the top there are about 1,000 steps.

Tourists may find it worth climbing when they stand at the top and look around. What a fantastic scene! Wanquan River is winding downward into the ocean like a jade belt. The rice fields are waving. The buffaloes are wandering about. You sure feel nice in breezes.

Guantang Hot Springs

Located at the foot of the Baishi Ridge, Guantang Hot Springs are rather rare in China. The heavy concentration of minerals such as sulfur and hydrogen sulfide creates a rather strong "rotten egg" smell, but the other minerals, which include fluorine, silicon, and strontium chloride, have such a pleasant effect on the skin and circulatory system that it is very easy to overlook this minor problem.

Water temperatures range from a pleasant 30℃ to a hot 45℃. Local residents have long used the hot springs to cure aches and pains, heart conditions, skin conditions, as well as chronic diseases. Medical experts in recent years have also explained the positive effects that bath therapy has on skin, the cardiovascular system, respiratory system, nervous system, as well as kidney function.

Jiaji Duck

Jiaji Duck is one of the four specialties of Hainan, but it has a unique history. Also known as "Muscovy Duck", Jiaji Duck originated in the Mexico and Brazil and was introduced to Hainan by overseas Chinese over 150 years ago.

Often force-fed, these ducks feature tender meat and thin crispy skin. The traditional way to prepare it is to boil it in water, dice it, then eat with mixture of vinegar, chopped ginger and sesame oil.

Hot-spring Goose

Hot-spring Goose is a hybrid kept by farmers living close to the Wanquan River. When the geese are small, farmers unleash them into the wild to hunt for their own food that is chiefly comprised of grass seeds. When the stage for putting on weight comes, farmers feed the geese a special diet.

Hot-spring Goose is nutritious, aromatic and delicious. Goose blood has a high concentration of protein and contains more than 10 rare elements such as iron, copper and calcium.

Fevervine Pasta

Fevervine is a kind of Chinese herb, with special smell and health benefits. Mixture of fevervine and marinated rice is ground into mushy liquid. Then dough is made after squeezing and kneading. After shaping the dough into small balls and boiling them with brown sugar, eggs, coconut slices and milk, the Fevervine Pasta is done. It's a very popular snack in summer in Hainan.

Hainan Mango Roll

The Hainan Mango Roll consists of fresh juicy slices of mango wrapped in a delicate rice noodle wrapper, and topped with mango jam. This dish is not only tasty, but also beautiful.

Notes:

1. The Bo'ao Forum for Asia is a non-profit organization that hosts high-level forums for leaders from government, business and academia in Asia and other continents to share their vision on the most pressing issues in this dynamic region and the whole world.

博鳌亚洲论坛是一个非营利组织，它为亚洲和其他国家领导人、企业界和学术界人士举办高层论坛，共同商讨本地动态区域乃至全世界最紧要的问题。

2. Located on the southern bank of the estuary of Wanquan River, Jade Belt Beach lies in east of Bo'ao Water-town and extends in a North-South direction, with only a narrow strip connected with land, just like a long "jade belt" that separates the Wanquan River from the South China Sea, forming a long and narrow natural beach.

玉带滩坐落于万泉河入海口南岸，博鳌水城以东，呈南北走向，只有一段狭窄的土地，就像一条长长的"玉带"。它将万泉河与南海隔开，形成一个狭长的天然海滩。

3. The female soldier stands upright, wearing the red army uniform, with a bamboo hat at her back, and a rifle on her shoulder. She wears grass shoes on her feet, with the bandage tied around her shanks.

这位身穿红军装的女战士挺拔地站着，背着斗笠，肩上扛着步枪，脚上穿着草鞋，小腿上扣着绑腿。

4. The heavy concentration of minerals such as sulfur and hydrogen sulfide creates a rather strong "rotten egg" smell, but the other minerals, which include fluorine, silicon, and strontium chloride, have such a pleasant effect on the skin and circulatory system that it is very easy to overlook this minor problem.

一些矿物如硫黄和硫化氢散发出较强的"臭鸡蛋"味道，但其他矿物，包括氟、硅、锶离子，对皮肤和血液循环有良好的疗效，所以常常忽略这小问题。

5. When the geese are small, farmers unleash them into the wild to hunt for their own food that is chiefly comprised of grass seeds.

农民们将小鹅崽放到野外觅食，吃草籽。

Chapter 5　Wanning

Wanning is located in the southeast of Hainan, 112 kilometers from Sanya in the south and 139 kilometers from Haikou in the north. It lies in the middle of Hainan's East Highway. The city occupies 1,883.3 square kilometers with a coastline of 109 kilometers. The whole population is about 570,000 according to the statistics in 2017. Like Wenchang, Wanning is also the hometown of many overseas Chinese in Southeast of Asia.

Wanning is characterized by a tropical monsoon climate, with little temperature variation. The region is usually very warm, with an average annual temperature of 24℃. Blessed with plenty of sunshine and rainfall, Wanning is a beautiful area in Hainan.

Wanning has some of the best surfing beaches in China, and has become a popular surfing destination. Wanning's Sun and Moon Bay and Shimei Bay are home to several surfing festivals and competitions yearly.

Dongshan Ridge

Known as First Mountain of Hainan Province, Dongshan Ridge is situated at the suburb of Wanning. It is 184 meters high, famous for "eight views of Dongshan Ridge". It is the oldest Buddhist shrine place in Hainan, and ranks national 3A-class tourist attraction.

Dongshan Ridge covers an area of 10 square kilometers, with southeast facing vast South China Sea. The Ridge has beautiful natural scenery, mysterious and unpredictable caves, winding valley and spring, and unique human landscape. The daedal hands of nature builds the magnificent eight views of Dongshan: Seven Gorges with Nested Cloud, Dignified Peak, Saint Boat Mooring, Penglai Fragrant Cave, Peering the Sea from Yaotai, Canopy Rosy Clouds, Cinnabar Water from Sea Hole, and Green Water Dragon Wandering.

The Buddha civilization of Dongshan Ridge has a long history. Temples and nunneries had been built since the Tang and Song Dynasties, which have attracted an endless stream of tourists and exuberant incense all year round.

In 748 AD, the famous monk Jianzhen headed eastward to Japan for the unsuccessful fifth time. Later, Jianzhen and his disciples reached Wanzhou (the current Wanning) after more than 40 days' hard trek. The day he arrived was a sunny day, with bird singing. All people came to escort Jianzhen and his team members. Master Lei Zhenhai led hundreds of monks chanting, which made the 62-year-old Jianzhen praise, "Now I'm on the Dongshan, I will rise again in the near future!" Then he led his disciples preaching and chanting in Dongshan for three days. Subsequently, Jianzhen went through hardships and returned to Yangzhou. He decided to start again, to sail eastward for the sixth time to Japan. He succeeded this time and later this initiative was called "making a comeback".

As early as in the Jin Dynasty, many poets and scholars had left many poems on the Dongshan Ridge stones, with Li, Kai, Xing and Cao style (four main Chinese ancient calligraphy fonts), which later accumulated into the Cliff-side carving groups. It can be called calligraphy encyclopedia attributing to its lavish calligraphy art works, eminent calligraphy art and long history. Its Cliff-side carving font has different sizes. Among them, the four Chinese characters of "Dong Shan Song Cui" carved on the Lingyun Cliff on the southside are the biggest stone inscriptions, whose characters are as high as 1.7 meters.

The cuisine of Dongshan Ridge is also well-known. Dongshan Mutton, Hele Mud Crab, Hou'an Mugil Cephalus, Dongshan Pancake, and Dongshan Partridge Tea are praised as "the five unique features of Dongshan". Thus people say "eating in Dongshan".

Xinglong Tropical Botanical Garden

Xinglong Tropical Botanical Garden can be a good place to get close to exotic experience. The garden is only 97 kilometers from Sanya and 176 kilometers from Haikou. It was built in 1957 and covers an area of 400,000 square kilometers. It possesses more than 1,200 plant species, such as coffee, pepper, cocoa, dragon trees, etc. Xinglong Tropical Botanical Garden is regarded as a hot destination and furthermore dedicated to issues related to botany and environmental protection in cooperation with agricultural authorities in China. Featuring tropical monsoon climate all year round, Xinglong Tropical Botanical Garden is suitable for tourism and thus evaluated as 4A-class tourism spot and model of agricultural tourism.

Featuring all sorts of plants, including coffee, pepper, cocoa, durian, mangosteen, antiaris toxicaria, Xinglong Tropical Botanical Garden domesticates tropical plants around the world and thus embodies a harmonious picture with plants. Besides, a bar counter is accessible to provide visitors many sorts of juice produced by the garden itself. The garden is divided into five functional areas: plant viewing area, experiment and demonstration area, research area, three-dimensional planting and breeding area, and ecological recreation area. Walking into the botanical garden is like opening an encyclopedia about tropical plants.

Xinglong Tropical Botanical Garden is nearly perfect for plants to grow. Now the botanical garden not only plays an important role as an agricultural base, but also is a famous tourist resort. It really deserves the name of "tropical plants encyclopedia". It is one of the most popular tourist attractions on Hainan Island.

Dazhou Island

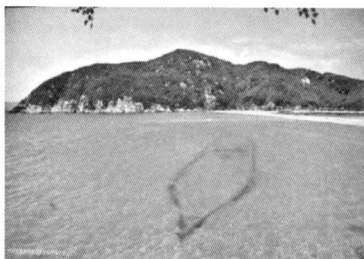

Dazhou Island lies in the southeast of Wanning, 15 kilometers away from the city. Covering an area of 4.36 square kilometers, Dazhou Island is made up of two smaller islands and three peaks, whose highest peak is 289.3 meters.

Dazhou Island is China's only production base for bird's nest, which is a Chinese delicacy known for its health benefits. Other wildlife abounds here, including pangolins, lizards, partridges, eagles, herons, petrels and more!

Dazhou Island is also a unique sightseeing destination, featuring a southern mountain and a northern mountain, with a 500-meter-long beach in between, which is submerged at high tide. With its amazingly clear water and beautiful mountain scenery,

Dazhou Island is a wonderful place to visit.

The island is also a national ocean nature reserve with colorful marine life, making it popular with water sports enthusiasts. Therefore, it is a great place for boating, diving, camping, swimming, fishing, and hiking.

Shenzhou Peninsula

Shenzhou used to stand for China. In fact, there is another meaning of Shenzhou, which refers to the place where the immortals live. So the Shenzhou Peninsula in Hainan is just like the fairyland where the gods live, beautiful and mysterious.

Shenzhou Peninsula is surrounded by the sea on three sides. The east-west end lies between the Laoye Sea and the South China Sea. As an inland sea, the Laoye Sea connects with the South China Sea at the west end. There are several mountains in different sizes on the peninsula. Due to the crustal force and wave erosion, five beautiful bays have been formed along the offshore of the peninsula. From east to west, they are Dongwo Bay, Liaoqian Bay, Wozi Bay, Xiwo Bay and Nanrong Bay.

Nanrong Bay is the most broad and connected land on the top of the peninsula. It has become the development site of many first-rate hotels and residential areas. The other bays are quieter and more plain. The beautiful natural environment makes it an ideal resort. At the same time, five-star hotels such as Sheraton Resort Hotel, Fupeng Hotel can meet the needs of many guests for seaside vacation.

In addition, the golf course is also very famous. The Shenzhou Golf Course is located on the east coast of Hainan Island. It has 36 holes and 5 practice holes. It is carefully designed by the famous International Golf Master Tom Weiskopf. The Tourist Resort has been rated as the best golf resort in the world in 2014, making it comparable to the high-end golf courses abroad.

Shimei Bay

Shimei Bay is a relatively new beach along the east coast of Hainan Island, about 15 kilometers to the nearest Xinglong town. Its beach is ideal to anyone who is looking for a real quiet, isolated beach resort. It is also a nice choice for golf players with 4 clubs. If you just want to lie on the beach, enjoy the crystal-clear water, sandy beach and resorts facilities, Shimei Bay is the best place to go.

Besides beach and pool, there are a lot to do during your stay: water sports, spa, cycling, wind surfing, reading or just lying on the beach with your favorite novel. You can also visit local areas by bike or take a tour to the biggest botanical garden, enjoy hot spring in Xinglong or play golf in the four golfing clubs nearby.

Hele Crab

Wanning provides a perfect home for Hele crabs, one of the well-known specialty dishes of Hainan. The shell of the Hele crab is green, but turns red when cooked. Inside the thin shells nestles delicate white crab meat and roe. It is often served with a dipping sauce made from ginger, garlic and vinegar, which brings out the amazing flavor of the crab meat. The best time for eating Hele crab is late summer and early fall.

Dongshan Mutton

Mutton is one of the most famous local specialties in Hainan. The local Dongshan goats are distinct from other breeds for their furs are uniformly black and their flesh is much tender, free from the usual unpleasant smell, because they are raised on the mountains.

Tender Zhegu tea-leaves on the mountain are the favorite food of the goats, so their meat is aromatic and non-greasy. It tastes delicious alone or can be made into a rich soup. It is often cooked with special seasoning and ingredients. With red color and savory taste, it is truly appealing and perfect to eat then served in hot pot.

Hou' an Rice Noodle

Hou' an Rice Noodle is the most famous breakfast in Wanning, and its restaurants are scattered around the city, even in Haikou and Sanya. The most important ingredient of Hou' an Rice Noodle is bone broth. It is made of fresh pig bones and pork offals with some pepper, which needs a long time for slow boiling. It is said that the chefs have to get up at 3 o' clock early in the morning to make the broth so that customers can have the best-quality rice noodle soup. Beside the soup, Hou' an Rice Noodle is well known for its distinct ingredients, such as the rice noodle, pork, pork offals, dried shrimp, green onion, and of course the famous Hainan lantern pepper.

Notes:

1. The daedal hands of nature builds the magnificent eight views of Dongshan: Seven Gorges with Nested Cloud, Dignified Peak, Saint Boat Mooring, Penglai Fragrant Cave, Peering the Sea from Yaotai, Canopy Rosy Clouds, Cinnabar Water from Sea Hole, and Green Water Dragon Wandering.

大自然的鬼斧神工造就了东山岭的八大景观：七峡巢云、正笏凌霄、仙舟系缆、蓬莱香窟、瑶台望海、冠盖飞霞、海眼流丹、碧水环龙。

2. As early as in the Jin Dynasty, many poets and scholars had left many poems on the Dongshan Ridge stones, with Li, Kai, Xing and Cao style (four main Chinese ancient calligraphy fonts), which later accumulated into the Cliff-side carving groups.

早在晋朝，许多文人墨客就在东山岭留下了大量以隶书、楷书、行书、草书（中国古代四大书法字体）书写的诗歌，后来形成悬崖石刻。

3. Featuring all sorts of plants, including coffee, pepper, cocoa, durian, mangosteen, antiaris toxicaria, Xinglong Tropical Botanical Garden domesticates tropical plants around the world and thus embodies a harmonious picture with plants.

兴隆热带植物园有各种各样的植物，包括咖啡、胡椒、可可、榴梿、山竹、见血封喉等，引进世界各地的热带植物，体现了植物和谐生长的画面。

4. Other wildlife abounds here, including pangolins, lizards, partridges, eagles, herons, petrels and more!

这里繁衍很多野生动物，包括穿山甲、蜥蜴、鹧鸪、老鹰、苍鹭、海燕等!

5. The local Dongshan goats are distinct from other breeds for their furs are uniformly black and their flesh is much tender, free from the usual unpleasant smell, because they are raised on the mountains.

因为养在山岭上，当地的东山羊与其他品种不同，毛黑均匀，肉质软嫩，没有难闻的膻味。

Chapter 6   Lingshui

Lingshui County extends 40 kilometers from north to south, 32 kilometers from east to west and covers a total land area of 1,128 square kilometers. It can be dated back to the sixth year of the Sui Dynasty (610 AD) and its established history has amounted almost to 1,400 years. On December 31st, 1987, the present county was set up and renamed Lingshui Li Minority Autonomous County.

Lingshui is honored with the titles of "Tropical Greenhouse", and "Tropical Plant Treasure Land" and has been China's first southern cultivation center. In winter, it is Hainan's vegetable base. Pearls nurtured in saltwater are the primary industries. In Lingshui there are abundant tropical fruits and economic farm products including coconut, lychee, longan, star fruit, dragon fruit, cherry tomato, banana, mango, watermelon, pepper, lantern pepper and betel nut.

Lingshui is rich in tourism resources. Natural features of the landscape include Coconut Island, Perfumed Bay, Tufu Bay, Nanwan Monkey Island, and the virgin tropical rainforest of Diaoluo Mountain.

Nanwan Monkey Island

Situated south of Lingshui, Nanwan Monkey Island is the only tropical island-type nature reserve for macaques—a state protected animal in China. Riding the ropeway, tourists will be delighted to find that they have a wonderful view of the ocean, the fishing rafts neatly placed by the bank and the

thick chains of mountains on the island with the birds gently singing and the monkeys' shouts reverberating around. Soon the mythical monkey island unfolds in front.

Built in 1965, the nature reserve has more than 2,000 monkeys now. Because of the wild environment, the island is regarded as the perfect paradise for monkeys.

Passing through a vegetation corridor, tourists will be amazed to find seven or eight macaques standing in a line along the path with triangular flags and saluting to welcome their honored guests. Some naughty ones are wandering with their flags in their hands, and even some are imitating their visitors' odd ways of walking. At times, young monkeys chase and fight with each other, and a stout one jumps into a pond from quite a tall tree with an excellent 360-degree turn in the air.

Apart from that, their swimming technique is quite superb. In the pond, some of them dive, some swim freestyle, and even some do the breaststroke. While watching, tourists will be amused and amazed, and can' t help applauding and clapping for them. In addition, tourists may also enjoy the circus performances by the monkeys. Of course, they can take photos with these cute monkeys and play with them. However, one must remember not to wear red clothes in order to avoid the naughty monkeys who might get annoyed, and be careful when feeding them.

Diaoluoshan National Rainforest Park

Diaoluoshan Mountain belongs to one of the most precious tropical rainforests in Hainan, with the highest altitude of 1,499 meters, almost the same height as Taishan Mountain.

Diaoluoshan Mountain mainly differs from others in its water, featuring with waterfalls, streams and ponds everywhere! The most famous one is the 100-meter-high Fengguoshan Waterfall cluster, which consists of four separate falls, namely, Xianlei Waterfall, Bingxin Waterfall, Sigui Waterfall and Caihong Waterfall. The changing season transforms the natural scenery of the waterfall throughout the year. The most magnificent fall is over 60 meters wide and has a maximum drop of more than 150 meters. It flows swiftly year round.

During the flood season, the force of the water shakes the ground beneath and pours down the falls like thousands of horses galloping, offering a breathtaking spectacle. Even in the dry season, the falls flow elegantly against the mountain. The plants around the pool bloom with various flowers that emanate an intoxicating fragrance.

With an average temperature of 20℃ and an annual rainfall of 2,160 millimeters, Diaoluoshan Mountain is a paradise for plants. There are 3,500 different kinds of plants and 250 species of flowers in the forest. Each year, from early spring, various kinds of flowers bloom one after another, including silk cotton, azalea, magnolia, round cardamom and phoenix flower. The forest is also a natural preserve of Chinese herbal medicines such as areca, agalloch, ganoderma and lucidum.

For those living in urban areas, wandering among the lakes and falls can give them a feeling of returning back to nature.

Boundary Island

Boundary Island is a small, pretty island located in the South Sea off Lingshui. It looks like a beauty floating in the sea, so local fishermen nicknamed it "Sleeping Beauty Island".

The eastern part of the island features sheer cliffs and white waves and foam dashing over the rocks on the shoreline. On the western side, there is a small beach with clean water, white sand and palm trees.

It takes only three minutes by yacht to get to the island. When the tide falls, one can catch crabs or pick up shells on the beach.

There are various odd-looking rocks on the island's hill, which is quite verdant with tropical plants. A granite-slate path on this island has the shapes and pictures of various ancient currency of China carved on it for tourist appreciation.

There are also entertainments and sports such as yachts, motorboats, sailboats, banana boats, or parasailing. Tourists can also enjoy tropical saltwater fish, various corals and rock formations on the island.

A large coral aquarium has been opened to the public on April 28th, 2013 at Boundary Island. Covering an area of 1,200 square meters, the aquarium features more than 10,000 coral samples and living corals, including staghorn, tubular and red and black corals. Visitors can also see the growing conditions of the corals. The opening of the aquarium is of great significance in promoting ocean knowledge among the public, and it can also contribute to research on the coral reef ecosystem.

Sour Rice Noodles

Sour rice noodles are one of characteristic snacks in Lingshui. It has a long history, which can be traced back to the Qing Dynasty. For the local people, the sour rice noodles are both snack and staple food. They eat them for breakfast every day or during festivals, and even entertain their guests. Unlike the Cantonese entertain their guests with terrific soup, the local people entertain their guests with unique sour rice noodles.

Lingshui sour rice noodles are white and smooth and appear thread-like. The rice noodles themselves are tasteless, but the spiced gravy makes them tasty. Each restaurant owners have their own unique skills to prepare the gravy, which is invitingly sweet and sour.

Noodle toppings are usually chopped chives, sesame oil, Hainan yellow chili sauce, fried peanuts, shredded pork meat and squid as well as some sliced dried beef. When dishing up, boiling spiced gravy is poured into the noodles. Finally, adding some boiling oil to maximize the flavor so as to make the noodle glossy and aromatic.

To enjoy this popular snack, you don't have to pick an expensive restaurant. Just look for little restaurants run by local people for authentic sour rice noodles at an economic price.

Notes:

1. In Lingshui there are abundant tropical fruits and economic farm products including coconut, lychee, longan, star fruit, dragon fruit, cherry tomato, banana, mango, watermelon, pepper, lantern pepper and betel nut.

陵水有丰富的热带水果和经济农作物，包括椰子、荔枝、龙眼、阳桃、火龙果、圣女果、香蕉、杧果、西瓜、胡椒、灯笼辣椒、槟榔。

2. Riding the ropeway, tourists will be delighted to find that they have a wonderful view of the ocean, the fishing rafts neatly placed by the bank and the thick chains of mountains on the island with the birds gently singing and the monkeys' shouts reverberating around.

乘坐索道，游客可愉悦地欣赏海景、岸边整齐的渔排、岛上层峦叠嶂的山脉，耳边回荡着鸟儿的轻声歌唱和猴子的叫声。

3. During the flood season, the force of the water shakes the ground beneath and pours down the falls like thousands of horses galloping, offering a breathtaking spectacle.

每逢洪水季节，流水震动山谷，好像万马奔腾，令人叹为观止。

4. Covering an area of 1,200 square meters, the aquarium features more than 10,000 coral samples and living corals, including staghorn, tubular and red and black corals.

水族馆占地面积1 200平方米，展出超过10 000种珊瑚标本和活珊瑚，包括鹿角状、管状和红、黑珊瑚。

5. Noodle toppings are usually chopped chives, sesame oil, Hainan yellow chili sauce, fried peanuts, shredded pork meat and squid as well as some sliced dried beef.

酸粉浇头通常是香葱，麻油，海南黄辣椒酱，炒花生，肉末，鱿鱼以及一些牛肉干。

Part Ⅵ   Western Part of Hainan

This part will focus on...

      · introduction to western part of Hainan;

      · Chengmai;

      · Lingao;

      · Danzhou;

      · Changjiang Li Autonomous County;

      · Dongfang.

Chapter 1 Introduction to Western Part of Hainan

The western part of Hainan consists of Danzhou, Dongfang, Ledong and other counties, where National Highway No. 225 and western highway run through. Located in a remote area with a sparse population, most of the tourist resources are still to be developed, and ordinary tourists seldom step their feet on this vast land. However, the scenery in the west is unique and different. In addition to the awesome sunshine, beach and sea as other coastal areas of the island, there are still many primitive forests and tropical rainforests. Among them, Jianfengling and Bawangling forests are state-level reserves, where vines are tangled and species are abundant. Many animals that have not been seen in other parts of the world are still living, such as gibbons, clouded leopards, king cobras, pangolins, large lizards and so on.

The tourism resources in the west are full of natural creation and have witnessed the culture passed down by ancestors. There are millennium salt fields, the oldest city in Hainan Island, Dongpo Academy, Jianfengling Tropical Rainforest Reserve, Datianpo Deer Reserve and so on.

Li and Miao ethnic groups have long lived on this primitive land and kept various mysterious customs including tattoos. With the opening of the Western Highway, it is convenient for people to come here for sightseeing. They can experience local unique ethnic culture and customs, such as boat houses, Li kilt, bamboo rice, Sanyuesan Festival.

The best time to travel is in winter. The climate along the western line is different from that elsewhere in Hainan. It's drier here. The temperature is the highest in Hainan. It can reach 38 degrees in summer. The rainfall is mainly concentrated in the typhoon season from June to November. In winter, because of the influence of ocean cold current, the temperature is relatively low and suitable for tourism.

Notes：

1. In addition to the awesome sunshine, beach and sea as other coastal areas of the island, there are still many primitive forests and tropical rainforests.

除了与本岛其他沿海地区一样拥有一级棒的阳光、沙滩和海水外，现在还保存着许多原始森林和热带雨林。

2. Many animals that have not been seen in other parts of the world are still living, such as gibbons, clouded leopards, king cobras, pangolins, large lizards and so on.

这里还生活着许多在世界其他地方已看不到的动物，如长臂猿、云豹、眼镜王蛇、穿山甲、大型蜥蜴等。

3. There are millennium salt fields, the oldest city in Hainan Island, Dongpo Academy, Jianfengling Tropical Rainforest Reserve, Datianpo Deer Reserve and so on.

这里有千年古盐田、海南岛最古老的城池、东坡书院、尖峰岭热带雨林保护区、以及大田坡鹿保护区等。

4. Li and Miao ethnic groups have long lived on this primitive land and kept various mysterious customs including tattoos.

黎、苗族同胞很久以前就以特有的方式生活在这片土地上，至今还保留着包括纹身在内的各种神秘习俗。

5. They can experience local unique ethnic culture and customs, such as boat houses, Li kilt, bamboo rice, Sanyuesan Festival.

他们可以体验船形屋、黎族筒裙、竹筒饭、农历三月三等当地特有的民族文化与风情。

Chapter 2   Chengmai

Situated in the northwest of Hainan Island and adjacent to Haikou, Chengmai has an area of 2,072 square kilometers. The County has a jurisdiction of 11 towns, 176 village committees and 867 natural villages with Town of Jinjiang as the County capital. Large areas of the county are covered by forest. The county is rich in selenium—a mineral essential for good health but required only in small amounts.

Chengmai had been honored as the "longevity hometown" of China and the world respectively in 2009 and 2012. Average life expectancy there is 77.79 years. According to the news report, the county has 215 centenarians from June, 2016 to April, 2017. Both the number of centenarians and their proportion in the overall population rank highest among all Chinese cities and counties.

Researches have been carried out to analyze the factors of longevity and have found the quality of drinking water in Chengmai to be high and rich in minerals. The soil is clean, meeting all national standards for soil quality. Rice, vegetables and fruit are rich in calcium, magnesium and selenium, and the county is well known for its high-quality coffee and oranges.

Mangrove Wetland Park

The 4A-level Mangrove Wetland Park in Chengmai has been opened to the public since August 23rd, 2015.

The park spans 2,200 acres of mangrove

forest, offering a variety of animal habitats and ecosystems to create an environmentally conscious, exciting experience for visitors. Tourists can have a look at the mangroves that grow in swamps and other aquatic plants, as well as animals like flamingos and many other kinds of birds.

The park has been designed with seven recreational areas, including a 4.2-km-long timber boardwalk, a mangrove wetland museum, a scenic restaurant and an amusement park for families, as well as other environmental education facilities.

Fushan Town

With its unique coffee charm, Fushan Town has been awarded the title of China's First Coffee Town by the China Fruit Marketing Association.

Fushan currently has a profitable coffee field of nearly 60,000 acres, with an annual production of 3,000 tons of beans.

In recent years, the town has also worked hard to combine coffee culture with tourism efforts to meet the increasing needs of the island's growing tourism industry and help more people be aware of the Fushan Coffee Town on Hainan Island.

With the Fushan Coffee Culture & Romance Town as the center, supporting facilities like a coffee research center, a world coffee brands trade center, and a coffee museum have been built in the town to integrate tourism elements from the world famous coffee industry and culture, and offer the tourists an one-stop world-class coffee, food and folk customs destination.

Meilang Twin Pagodas

The Meilang Twin Pagodas are situated on the southeastern side of Meilang Village, Meiting Town. The pagodas were built around 800 years ago during the early Yuan Dynasty and have been popularly known as the Sister Pagodas.

Government records from the Ming Dynasty stated that the pagodas were built by a local man named Chen Daoxu in memory of his two daughters Chen Lingzhao and Chen Shanzhang, both of whom were devout Buddhists. The pagodas originally stood in front of the Jirui Nunnery, where Chen Shanzhang resided as a nun. The Jirui Nunnery had fallen into ruin long ago but the pagodas survive as one of the few reminders of its existence.

The pagodas have been renowned for their elaborate stone carvings and exquisite stonework. The images are very lifelike and reflect secular life during the late Song and early Yuan Dynasties. The pagodas can be considered unique for several reasons: Firstly, the entire body of the pagodas has been constructed by basalt from northern Hainan's volcanic region. Secondly, the structures are put together using mortise and tenon joints, and the stones overlap without binding. Although the buildings have suffered from various stages of degradation, the structures as a whole are intact, making them rare for pagodas in China of similar age.

Yongqing Temple

Located in Chengmai, Yongqing Temple is surrounded by gardens. Being the largest Buddhist temple in the north of Hainan, Yongqing Temple is rated as "the temple with the most Buddhas" by Shanghai Guinness World Records. There is a total of 42 Buddha statues in the temple, all made of white jade, including Sakyamuni, the Lying Buddha, the Thousand Hands Guanyin, and the Wenshu Bodhisattva.

Yongqing Temple was first built in the Song Dynasty, and later expanded to the current size. The temple was once visited by Su Dongpo, the famous poet in the Song Dynasty, who wrote the temple's serene beauty.

Currently, the temple enjoys great prestige not only for its Buddhist significance, but also for its picturesque surroundings. This area features ample sunshine, sea, sand, flower blossoms, and greenery. Visitors can feel the peace and harmony of Buddhist culture here and experience the joy of returning to nature.

Ruixi Zongzi

Ruixi Zongzi is filled with pork of organic black pigs enjoying a chewier texture and a stronger flavor. It also has a strict wrapping procedure, making it delicious and good-looking.

Zongzi is an important festival snack to family and friends for annual Dragon Boat Festival.

Sticky Rice Cakes

This popular pastry in Chengmai is made from a sticky rice paste, filled with shredded coconut, crushed peanut, sesame oil, and sugar. The recipe has been passed down through generations, and it is eaten at every gathering and festival. Often served wrapped in a strip of banana or palm leaf, this snack is chewy and sweet.

Ruixi Beef Jerky

Ruixi Beef Jerky is a well-loved snack. The beef jerky is seasoned with sugar and is usually made from a large slice of beef. Visitors can try some of the most tempting Ruixi Beef Jerky at the Ruixi Food Street where all kinds of traditional and tasty Chengmai snacks are available. Most of snacks are freshly made, without preservatives.

Kuding Tea

In Hainan, Kuding Tea originates from Chengmai. Commonly known as Chading, Fuding and Gaolu tea, it is a popular health drink in Hainan with its bitter-sweet taste.

The tea has long been associated with having traditional Chinese medicinal

properties. It has been listed as valuable Chinese medicine as early as the Yuan, Ming, and Qing Dynasties for its beneficial effects to the eyes, heart, brain, and stomach. Therefore, it has been dubbed as "healthy tea" "beauty care tea" "slimming tea" "anti-hypertensive tea", and "longevity tea".

Notes:

1. The park has been designed with seven recreational areas, including a 4. 2-km-long timber boardwalk, a mangrove wetland museum, a scenic restaurant and an amusement park for families, as well as other environmental education facilities.

公园设计了七个娱乐区，其中包括一条4.2公里长的木栈道、红树林湿地博物馆，风味餐厅和家庭娱乐园，以及其他环境教育设施。

2. Secondly, the structures are put together using mortise and tenon joints, and the stones overlap without binding.

其二，建筑结构采用榫眼凹凸相接，条石叠垒不粘合。

3. There is a total of 42 Buddha statues in the temple, all made of white jade, including Sakyamuni, the Lying Buddha, the Thousand Hands Guanyin, and the Wenshu Bodhisattva.

寺中共有42尊佛像，全部由汉白玉制成，包括卧佛释迦牟尼，千手观音和文殊菩萨。

4. This popular pastry in Chengmai is made from a sticky rice paste, filled with shredded coconut, crushed peanut, sesame oil, and sugar.

澄迈这种热门糕点是用糯米糊做成的，内馅有椰丝、花生碎、芝麻油和糖。

5. Therefore, it has been dubbed as "healthy tea" "beauty care tea" "slimming tea" "anti-hypertensive tea", and "longevity tea".

因此，它被誉为"健康茶""美容茶""减肥茶""降压茶""长寿茶"。

Chapter 3   Lingao

Lingao is situated in the northwest of Hainan Island. It borders Chengmai to the east and Danzhou to the south with the Qiongzhou Strait to the north. The county has a land area of 1,317 square kilometers, 10 towns, 154 villages, 17 neighborhood committees, 733 rural villages and two state-owned farms.

Lingao is rich in natural land resources, possessing level terrain, fertile soil and an abundance of rainfall; all of these are available for the development of agriculture. Crops grown here include rice from the numerous paddy fields, rubber, sugar cane, lychee, banana and many others. Roasts Suckling Piglet, Duowen Water Spinach and many other agricultural products are famous both home and abroad.

Lingao has a coastline stretching 114.7 kilometers with 11 good natural harbors including Jinpai, Xinying, Diaolou and Huanglong, which has mudflats extending to 5,333 hectares that provide favorable conditions for the development of maritime aquaculture and ocean fishing.

Unique local conditions and customs have turned Lingao into a "National Folk Art Village". Both the fishermen's melody "Beautiful Lili" and the local puppet show originated from Lingao.

Compared with other counties, Lingao does not have many sightseeing sites. Some of the tourism resources include the Lingao Cape, Gaoshan ridges, and Confucius Temple.

Lingao Cape

Lingao Cape is situated in the north of Lingao and separated from Leizhou Peninsula. Lingao Cape is in a prominent headland in Qiongzhou Strait. It is surrounded by the sea and has a long coastline of 7 kilometers. The beach is soft and white, thus making a good natural bathing beach. There is a lighthouse, customs sites of the Qing Dynasty, beacon ruins of the Ming Dynasty and other relics and monuments.

Lingao Cape is of historic significance. It was one of the main sites that the Chinese People's Liberation Army landed successively in Hainan Island in 1950. To commemorate this campaign and the soldiers who died heroically, a Liberation Park had been built, and now it has become one of the important patriotic education bases where a large number of students come to show their respect yearly.

Lingao Roast Suckling Piglet

Lingao Roast Suckling Piglet is a must-try dish for each visitor coming to Lingao.

The piglets are raised by local farmers who always unleash them into the wild to hunt down their own food that chiefly comprises of grass seeds. They usually weigh approximately 10 kilograms.

The tasty dish can be prepared in many ways such as steamed, sauté and barbecued, but the best way to cook them is to roast them so the skin gets really crispy. The suckling piglets are widely available at local restaurants, either served in whole or in well-cut slices with some special homemade sweet and sour sauce.

During the food preparation, the chef will butcher the piglet well, remove the bones and season well before placing it over a simmering charcoal fire. The meat is then frequently flipped and basted with peanut oil. It is said that this cooking method results in the suckling piglet's skin becoming crisp but not spongy, as well as adding to the appearance and flavor.

The roast sucking piglet is favored by local people and visitors for their crisp skin, fine meat, soft bones and an appetizing smell, and has been named as one of Top Ten Fantastic Dishes in Hainan in 2012.

Lingao's Puppet Plays

Lingao's Puppet Plays together with human actors are full of local characteristics. It is said that this puppet plays made its appearance even earlier than Qiong Opera. It is distinct from puppet of other cities or counties: there's no curtain on the stage, and the puppet and its manipulator play the same role. The chief accompanying music is produced by double suona horn (a Chinese traditional instrument). The actors make themselves up and then show on the stage with the puppet.

The puppet is finely made. With moving eyes and mouth, the puppets look as if they had life. On the stage actors and the puppets need to coordinate well, and each actor manipulates one puppet and performs the role in the play.

Because of its special local feature and different presentation, this kind of puppet play has gained lots of local fans.

Notes:

1. Lingao is rich in natural land resources, possessing level terrain, fertile soil and an abundance of rainfall; all of these are available for the development of agriculture.

临高县自然土地资源丰富、地势平坦、土壤肥沃、降雨量充沛，适合发展农业。

2. Lingao has a coastline stretching 114.7 kilometers with 11 good natural harbors including Jinpai, Xinying, Diaolou and Huanglong, which has mudflats extending to 5,333 hectares that provide favorable conditions for the development of maritime

aquaculture and ocean fishing.

临高县海岸线长达 114.7 公里，拥有 11 个包括金牌、新盈、调楼和黄龙等的天然良港，滩涂连绵 5 333 公顷，为发展海水养殖、海洋捕捞业提供了优越条件。

3. Unique local conditions and customs have turned Lingao into a "National Folk Art Village". Both the fishermen's melody "Beautiful Lili" and the local puppet show originated from Lingao.

独特的风土人情造就了临高这样一个"民间艺术之乡"，渔歌《哩哩美》和人偶戏均出自临高。

4. The piglets are raised by local farmers who always unleash them into the wild to hunt down their own food that chiefly comprises of grass seeds.

当地农民总是采用野外放养的方式饲养小猪，让小猪自己觅食、吃草籽。

5. It is distinct from puppet of other cities or counties: there's no curtain on the stage, and the puppet and its manipulator play the same role.

临高木偶戏与其他市县的木偶戏迥然不同：舞台上没有幕布，木偶和它的操控者饰演同一角色。

Chapter 4   Danzhou

Situated in the northwest of Hainan Island, Danzhou adjoins Lingao, Chengmai on the east, Qiongzhong on the southeast, and Baisha and Changjiang on the southwest.

The city covers a total area of 3,394 square kilometers. Nada Town is the economic and cultural center as well as the transportation hub of the western part of Hainan province.

Danzhou has a long history and is rich in tourist resources. Its main scenic spots include Dongpo Academy, Hainan Tropical Botanical Garden, Songtao Reservoir, Geological Park of Stone Flower Caves, Lanyang Hot Spring, Roaring Waves at Longmen, Millennium Ancient Salt Fields and Yangpu Port.

As the western route of expressway runs through the city, Danzhou is the hub of land communications in the western part of Hainan Province. Nada Town, the urban area of Danzhou, is 137 kilometers from Haikou on the east and 284 kilometers from Sanya on the south. Bus lines from the city extend to every city and town of the Island as well as to Guangzhou in Guangdong Province.

Dongpo Academy

Located in the Zhonghe Town of Danzhou, Dongpo Academy ranked national 3A-level scenic spot in July 2011. It has been a national key cultural relic protection site. The history of this academy could be dated back to the Song Dynasty. In 1097, government official Su Dongpo was demoted from Huizhou to Danzhou, staying there for over three years. During this period of time, he made acquaintance with local people, delivered lectures, and spread the culture of the mainland. In honor of his great deeds, an academy was built on the original site.

The gate of the academy faces south, imposing, grand and quaint. Four Chinese characters "东坡书院" (Dongpo Academy) was written horizontally at the top, whose inscription was made by the successful candidate in the imperial examinations at the provincial level named Zhang Ji in the Qing Dynasty. Its main attraction—Zai Jiu Tang in Chinese, is the second-row courtyard where Su Dongpo gave lectures and met with his friends. In the lobby, east and west wings are displayed piles of Su's works of calligraphy, paintings, and historic manuscripts. There is a courtyard between Zai Jiu Tang and the lobby, with corridors and houses on east and west wings, which forms a courtyard with houses on four sides. In the courtyard stands a mango tree with hundreds of years old, dense and flouring, so the whole courtyard seems very quiet and solemn.

Hainan Tropical Botanical Garden

Hainan Tropical Botanical Garden is located in the western suburbs of Nada Town, Danzhou, the herbarium parks on Danzhou Campus of the Hainan University (formerly the South China University of Tropical Agriculture), and the Chinese Academy of Tropical Agriculture Science. It covers 32 hectares, and was founded in 1958. The park has more than 1,000 kinds of rare tropical plants from over 40 countries, being the treasure house of tropical plant resources in China and a microcosm of the world's tropical crop

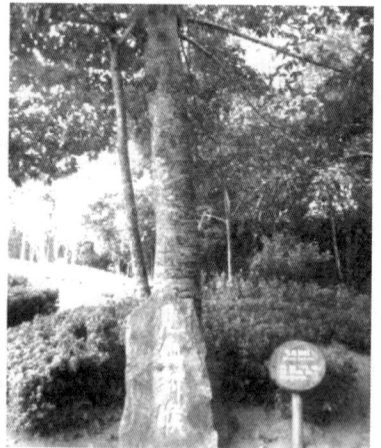

resources. The garden has seven zones represented by the existing precious tropical plants: the tropical spice plants, the tropical medicinal plants, the tropical fruits, the tropical oil plants, the tropical ornamental plants and so on.

Songtao Reservoir

Songtao Reservoir is located in the upstream of Nandu River, across three counties of Danzhou, Baisha and Qiongzhong. Honored as the Pearl of the Island, it is the source of drinking water for all Hainan people and one of the ten national reservoirs.

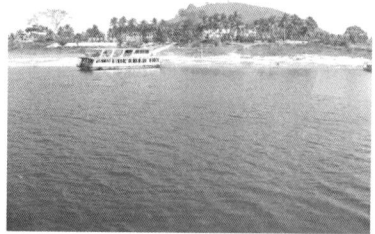

It was first built in 1958 and the construction was carried on for 10 years. It is also one of the largest earth dam projects in China. The dam is 80.1 meters high and 760 meters long, intercepting the roaring Nandu River water in the Nanfengyang and the Fanjiayang river valleys. The Songtao Reservoir is 144 square kilometers in surface, and has many inner islands. With a volume of 3,340 million cube meters, the dam stores rainfall from an area of 1,400 square meters on both sides of the Nandu River, comprising an overall irrigation system and supplying water to large pieces of farm land in the north and northwest of Hainan Island.

Huge Songtao Lake is surrounded by mountains and tropical rainforests. The lake is good for agriculture, fishery and industry. However, to protect the source of the drinking water, a tour of luxury cruise ship on the lake is not available any more, neither can tourists enjoy the delicious local fish on the lake.

Geological Park of Stone Flower Caves

Geological Park of Stone Flower Caves is situated at the foot of Yingdao Mountain in the State-owned Bayi Farm, only 28 kilometers away from Danzhou.

In Geological Park of Stone Flower Caves, there is a dry cave and a flooded cave which experts confirm they were formed around 1.4 million years ago.

The dry cave has a length of some 1.5 kilometers of which so far only around 510 meters have been explored. Within its interior there are stalactites, stalagmites, stone pillars, stone flags, stone waterfalls, curled emery stones, aragonite flowers and single crystal calcite flowers. All of these are extremely ornamental and of great interest as the shapes of the curled stones seem to be spectacular. Experts credit the stones with national level since aragonite flowers and single crystal calcite flowers are rarely seen either at home or abroad.

The flooded cave is three kilometers long, and at present about 250 meters have been explored. At its deepest point, the water in the cave is seventeen meters deep with a cave width varying between three and fifteen meters. The interior of the flooded cave has a peculiar shape with a huge stalactite joining the top of the cave to the floor. This is similar in appearance to the mythical Dragon King of the Eastern Sea's heavenly needle. Nothing more beautiful can be imagined than a tour by boat through the cave which is just like the Dragon King's Palace!

Lanyang Hot Spring

Located in Lanyang Farm, Lanyang Hot Spring is one of the largest hot springs in Hainan, with 2,000 tons of daily flow. There are tens of natural spring mouths with average temperature of 78.4℃. The spring contains rich healthy elements such as zinc, strontium, lithium and bromine.

Proper spring bathing can have some beneficial therapy effect to neurasthenia, cardiovascular and rheumatic diseases. There are both hot spring and cold spring in Lanyang. It is surprising that the space between mouths of hot spring and cold spring is only one meter.

This place has been developed into a holiday resort with complete facilities, comfortable environment and magnificent landscapes full of flowers and fruit trees. It is really worth tasting local special food like hotpot in hot spring and spring boiled eggs.

Roaring Waves at Longmen

The Longmen Hill is one of the famous attractions in the volcanic coast along the seaside at E' man Town of Danzhou. The Longmen Hill is composed of rock, standing along the coast, with the highest point of 39 meters. Looking from north to south, its peaks stretch long and unbroken, creating a quite spectacular view. It looks just like the Great Wall. The gate on the east side of hill has a reputation—the First Door to South Sky, and is more than 30 meters high, 20 meters wide. When the north wind is blowing, the huge waves strike the rock gate. The sound, like beating drums, resounds across over ten miles. That is the origin for "Roaring Waves at Longmen".

According to the historical record of Danzhou, Fu Nanshe, the leader of Li Group in the Ming Dynasty, settled down there with his troop after suffering a setback in uprising. They fought with official armies for over ten years at the place. Roaring Waves at Longmen has gained its name from the Ming Dynasty and has been admired by visitors since then.

Millennium Ancient Salt Fields

The Millennium Ancient Salt Fields remained till today respectively in Yangpu Peninsula and at E' man Town. The former has a total area of 50 hectares, which has more than 7,300 different patterns of inkstone-shaped salt trough, and an annual output of 500 tons. The latter has an area of about 66.67 hectares, with an annual output of 800 tons.

According to the legend 1,200 years ago, a group of workers who wanted to extract salt from sea water moved to Yangpu Peninsular from Fujian Province and discovered new methods of making salt by chance. Then they made a great achievement by drilling rocks to make containers for sea water and exposing them in the sun. In this way, salt is being extracted from sea water.

Up to now, the local villagers are making salt in the same way. Tourists can go closer to the salt fields and observe the process of making salt. They can also taste the local characteristic dish—salt-roasted chicken.

Danzhou Zongzi

Zongzi is a traditional Chinese food, made of glutinous rice stuffed with different fillings and wrapped in bamboo, reed, or other large flat leaves. They are cooked by steaming or boiling. They are traditionally eaten during the Dragon Boat Festival which falls on the fifth day of the fifth month of the lunar calendar.

Hainan Zongzi is larger than other types, with large amounts of fillings. In Hainan, Zongzi fillings can include chicken, pork, salted duck egg, shrimp, shredded squid, and more. Danzhou Zongi fillings are even more varied, including sea salt, red snapper, and other varieties. They share some important qualities though— they are always tender, flavorful, and made with high quality rice and plenty of fillings.

Danzhou Zongzi has enjoyed high reputation in Hainan Island and they are often sent as gifts to friends or relatives in the season of Dragon Boat Festival.

Notes：

1. There is a courtyard between Zai Jiu Tang and the lobby, with corridors and houses on east and west wings, which forms a courtyard with houses on four sides.

载酒堂和大堂相隔一庭院，东西两侧是廊舍，与载酒堂相接，形成一个四合院。

2. The garden has seven zones represented by the existing precious tropical plants: the tropical spice plants, the tropical medicinal plants, the tropical fruits, the tropical oil plants, the tropical ornamental plants and so on.

园区由珍贵热带乔木组成，分布在七大区域：热带香料植物、热带药用植物、热带水果、热带油料植物、热带观赏植物等。

3. Honored as the Pearl of the Island, it is the source of drinking water for all Hainan people and one of the ten national reservoirs.

松涛水库被誉为宝岛明珠，是海南人民的饮用水源，也是全国十大水库之一。

4. Within its interior there are stalactites, stalagmites, stone pillars, stone flags, stone waterfalls, curled emery stones, aragonite flowers and single crystal calcite flowers.

水花石洞里有钟乳石、石笋、石柱、石旗、石瀑布、卷曲的金刚石、文石花、单晶方解石花。

5. When the north wind is blowing, the huge waves strike the rock gate. The sound, like beating drums, resounds across over ten miles. That is the origin for "Roaring Waves at Longmen".

北风刮来时，巨浪冲击着石门，声音像击鼓声，响彻十里，这就是"龙门激浪"的来源。

Chapter 5   Changjiang Li Autonomous County

Changjiang Li Autonomous County, the hometown of mango in China, is located in the northwest of Hainan, adjacent to mountains and sea. The county people's government is stationed in Shilu Town, 196 kilometers away from Haikou, and 220 kilometers away from Sanya. Scenic spots include Ancient Changhua City, Changhua Ridge, Qixing Yanwo Ridge, Bawangling Nature Reserve, Qiziwan Bay, Futou Mountain Nature Reserve, etc. Ancient Changhua City is a famous historic resort, located on the west coast of Changjiang River. Bawangling Nature Reserve, covering an area of more than 6,600 hectares, lies in the southeast of the county. It is the only nature reserve for gibbons in China. With an average annual temperature of 24.3℃, Changjiang enjoys good ecological environment, fertile land and abundant water resources. It is suitable for tourism in all seasons.

Bawangling Nature Reserve

Resources of Bawangling tropical forest are abundant, well preserved and of great potential for development. It is famous for its typicality, uniqueness and diversity.

The vegetation mainly consists of low mountain rain forest, valley rainforest and mountain rainforest. Valley rainforests are little and massive in the valley terrain of 400 to 800 meters; low mountain rainforests are distributed below 600 meters; mountain rainforests are distributed under various topographic conditions of 600 to 1000 meters.

The main vegetation types in the garden are Lauraceae, Fagaceae, Alphaceae, Rubiaceae and Siraitiaceae. The park is an exhibition hall of the tropical rainforest. The characteristics of the tropical rainforest can be seen everywhere, such as "upright roots like boards" "old stems with flowers" "sky gardens" "single tree forests" "epiphytes capable of climbing" "twining and strangling plants".

Yajia Waterfall Group consists of the grand waterfalls and the wavy rocks. The elevation difference of the grand waterfalls is 150 meters, with a width of about 30 meters. There is a deep pond at the bottom of the waterfalls, which is about 5 meters deep, 30 meters long and 20 meters wide. The top of the waterfall is a cascade waterfall group, with a total of 5 cascades and a drop of 2 to 20 meters.

Qiziwan Bay

Qiziwan Bay is situated in the west of Changjiang River. It is adjacent to Changhua Ridge in the east and connects the sea in the west. The coast line is about 20 kilometers long, looking like an S shape. The water here is clear and the sand is fine, soft, and white as silver. There are lots of strange rocks, verdant trees, and beautiful mountains along the coast. It is an amazing natural bathing place, and also an ideal place for sunbathing and sand bathing.

The most attractive of Qiziwan Bay is its natural barrier, i. e. a sailboat stone, which separates the inner lake from the open sea. The visitors may feel amazed that the waves inside are rather calm, while the waves outside are magnificent. A stream originating from Changhua Mountains, turns back and forth through mountains into the bay and enters the sea. The running water is not dry all the year round. It has become a natural freshwater bathing place. The spring water contains high-quality sulfur minerals and can treat skin diseases.

When you have a bird's eye-view of the sea, the arc of the beach is like a giant basket. Red, blue, green, yellow, purple, or colorful stones are scattered along the bay. They look like chess falling on the beach. Moreover, there are other beautiful natural landscapes in the Bay, and it is a perfect spot for viewing the sunset.

Qixing Yanwo Ridge

Qixing Yanwo Ridge is well-known for its charming scenery, green mountains, and hot springs. Its peak is 487 meters high. Changhua River surges in front of the ridge, while hot springs keep running behind the ridge.

At the southern end of the ridge, there is a huge cliff, under which there is a large circular cave, which is the habitat for swallows. Thousands of swallows build nests in the crevices, multiply and thrive, so the name of Yanwo Ridge was given. Every morning, swallows fly out of the cave in droves in search of food, and return to their nests in the sunset, so in the morning and evening, swallows swirl densely on the mountains, often causing a spectacle view that resembles a dark overcast sky.

In the cave, a variety of stalactites are everywhere, colorful and magnificent. At the foot of the west ridge, there is a small village of Li ethnic people. Looking from afar, the mountain and the small village form a harmonious picture. Villagers have a long history of protecting the birds, so that the bird's cave has never been harassed.

There are hot springs with seven holes behind the ridge, so it is named "Seven Star Springs". The spring pool is 10 meters long and 7 meters wide. The depth of the pool is more than 1 meter. The surface of the pool is more than 100 square meters. There is a simple bathing pool, which can accommodate more than 400 people to bathe every day. It is said that it is rich in sulfur minerals and can treat many skin diseases. Moreover, the water temperature is suitable for bathing so many people come to enjoy the hot spring all the year round.

Changjiang Mangoes

Changjiang is the largest mango base in Hainan Province with the largest area, the highest yield, the most varieties, the best quality and the fairest prices. It ranks top three of the mango counties nationwide. It is known as "the land of mango" and is well-known throughout China and even the world.

As early as a thousand years ago, Changjiang had begun the history of mango planting. On this ancient land, there have been nearly 3,000 native mango trees for hundreds of years. In the late 1970s, Changjiang began to introduce improved varieties of mango, which opened a new era of scientific mango cultivation. In 2000, it entered the peak period of mango planting, and nearly 100,000 mu of mango was planted in the county.

Mangoes grown in Changjiang enjoy beautiful appearance, high sweetness, and good quality. Every year, Changjiang launches "Mango Tourist Month", which attracts many tourists to pick mangoes in orchards. During the promotion, besides the pleasure of picking and tasting mango, visitors can visit the mango processing and production bases, watch the centuries-old mango trees and the traditional custom performances of Li nationality. They can also participate in the interactive activities of tourists and appreciate the exhibition of photographic works of art on mangoes.

Notes:

1. Scenic spots include Ancient Changhua City, Changhua Ridge, Qixing Yanwo Ridge, Bawangling Nature Reserve, Qiziwan Bay, Futou Mountain Nature Reserve, etc.

风景名胜区内包含古昌化城、昌化岭、七星燕窝岭、霸王岭自然保护区、棋子湾、斧头山自然保护区等景点。

2. The park is the exhibition hall of the tropical rainforest. The characteristics of the tropical rainforest can be seen everywhere, such as "upright roots like boards" "old stem with flowers" "sky gardens" "single tree forests" "epiphytes capable of climbing" "twining and strangling plants".

公园是热带雨林的展览馆，热带雨林所特有的"直立如屏的板状根""老茎生花""空中花园""独木成林""能攀善爬的附生植物""缠绕绞杀植物"等特征随处可见。

3. The most attractive of Qiziwan Bay is its natural barrier, i. e. a sailboat stone, which separates the inner lake from the open sea.

棋子湾最吸引人的是它的天然屏障，比如"帆船石"，把湾内外分割开来。

4. Thousands of swallows build nests in the crevices, multiply and thrive, so the name of Yanwo Ridge was given.

成千上万的燕子在石壁缝隙筑窝，繁衍生息，燕窝岭因此得名。

5. Changjiang is the largest mango base in Hainan Province with the largest area, the highest yield, the most varieties, the best quality and the fairest prices.

昌江是海南省种植面积最大、产量最高、品种最多、品质最优、价格适宜的杧果大县。

Chapter 6　Dongfang

Located in the southwest of Hainan Island, Dongfang covers an area of 2,272 square kilometers and has a population of 463,000. The climate here is pleasant, with an annual average temperature of 25℃. Thanks to the abundant sunshine and unique minerals, Dangfang is the hometown of the precious and rare scented rosewood. As the saying goes, the best scented rosewood in the world is cultivated in China, while the scented rosewood in Dongfang tops the list, especially that from E' xian Ridge, which can be regarded as a natural treasure.

The transport is convenient, for high-speed railway around the island and National Highway No. 225 run across the city. The tourism resources are rich, with rivers, lakes, seas, forests and springs. Famous scenic spots include Yulinzhou Beach, Sibiwan Bay, Daguangba Reservoir, E' xian Ridge, Datian Thamin Deer Reserve.

When you come to Dongfang, Sigeng roast suckling pig is a must-eat delicacy. Pitaya is the characteristic fruit of the city. It is one of the healthy fruits and has promising economic value. There is a largest winter chrysanthemum base in China.

Yulinzhou Sandbar

Yulinzhou Sandbar is located on the seashore of Basuo Port. It had been listed as one of the eight scenic spots in Hainan during the reign of Kangxi in the Qing Dynasty. There is a hill with all kinds of bare rocks. Because of the overlapping rocks, the

sandbar in the sun shines like fish scales, so it is called "Fish Scale Islet".

When you come to the beach of Yulinzhou, the clear, green water and the turning windmill will make you feel much better. The rocks on the seashore are pounded by the waves all the year round, forming various shapes of strange rocks, some of which are like umbrella tops, some of which look like capes, some of which are magnificent and arrogant, some of which are beautiful and soft, some of which are above the sea surface, some of which lie on the side of the beach…It's really beautiful, of course, the mood is also cheerful for them.

The lighthouse on the sandbar is the beacon for giant ships and fishing boats to sail back and forth. This is the landmark and symbol of city and the hope of fishermen. No matter how dark the night is, they can always see the dim light.

It's said that the most romantic thing in the city is to see the sunset on the sandbar, for one can have an intoxicating view of the sunset by the sea.

Daguangba Scenic Area

Daguangba Scenic Area is famous for the reservoir and power station, which is the second largest in Hainan. The surface of the reservoir covers 100 square kilometers, with a beautiful scenery of lakes and mountains. Daguangba Hydropower Station ranks the largest earth dam in Asia with a huge momentum. Its length is nearly 6 kilometers, its elevation is 144 meters and its capacity is 240,000 kilowatts. This is the earliest hydroelectric site in China, which has become a historical site witnessing Japan's invasion of China and plundering of China's resources. It is also known as the natural park of the city. It has received a large number of domestic and foreign tourists. The comprehensive development of tourism is very advantageous.

Sigeng Roast Suckling Pig

Besides the beautiful scenery, there is also one delicacy—Sigeng Roast Suckling Pig. Many tourists come to the city just for a taste of the roast suckling pigs. It is said that Sigeng Roast Suckling Pigs are better than those around the island. The little piglets are kept in the open and fed small fish and rice gruel. The exquisite recipe also adds glamour to this delicacy. First of all, pickle with onion, garlic, ginger, sauce, aged wine and other special spices for several hours, and then roast it on charcoal, until the skin is sauce-red. To enjoy the crisp pigskin, it is strongly recommended to dip it in sugar or in special sweet and sour sauce.

Notes:

1. As the saying goes, the best scented rosewood in the world is cultivated in China, while the scented rosewood in Dongfang tops the list, especially that from E' xian Ridge, which can be regarded as a natural treasure.

正如俗话所说的, 世界花梨看中国, 海南东方花梨最上乘, 尤其是俄贤岭的黄花梨, 堪称自然界瑰宝。

2. Famous scenic spots include Yulinzhou beach, Sibiwan Bay, Daguangba Reservoir, E' xian Ridge, Datian Thamin Deer Reserve.

著名景点包括鱼鳞洲、四必湾、大广水库、俄贤岭、大田坡鹿保护区。

3. It had been listed as one of the eight scenic spots in Hainan during the reign of Kangxi in the Qing Dynasty.

它在清朝康熙年间就被列为海南八大风景之一了。

4. It's said that the most romantic thing in the city is to see the sunset on the sandbar, for one can have an intoxicating view of the sunset by the sea.

有人说，在东方能想到的最浪漫的事，就是在鱼鳞洲看夕阳无限好。

5. This is the earliest hydroelectric site in China, which has become a historical site witnessing Japan's invasion of China and plundering of China's resources.

这里有中国最早的水电站遗址，是日本侵华掠夺我国资源的历史见证。

Part VII Central Part of Hainan

This part will focus on...

- introduction to central part of Hainan;

- Tunchang;

- Qiongzhong Li and Miao Autonomous County;

- Wuzhishan;

- Baoting Li and Miao Autonomous County.

Chapter 1   Introduction to Central Part of Hainan

Central part of Hainan includes Tunchang, Baisha, Qiongzhong, Wuzhishan and Baoting. The majority of people who live in these areas are the Li and Miao nationalities, where tourists can visit the unique boat-shape houses built by the Li people, enjoy the local dishes such as the bamboo rice, the shanlan rice wine, or observe the local festivals.

The Department of Culture and Sports of Hainan Province announced on August 21st, 2015 that Hainan Province has planned to integrate resources in Baoting, Baisha, Qiongzhong, Wuzhishan, Tunchang and Ding' an to build a central cultural tourism green belt involving ecological culture, culture of Li and Miao nationalities, mountain sports and rural culture, so as to promote the integration and development of central cultural tourism.

According to the initiative, the above six cities and counties in central part of Hainan are natural scenic regions for ecological and cultural tourism, thanks to a beautiful ecological environment, breathtaking mountains, fresh air, birdsong, and flowers. There are 22 ecological and cultural scenic areas under construction or expansion, including Maogan Ecological Tourism Area in Baoting, Butterfly Ecological Gardens in Wuzhishan, cliff inscriptions cluster in Shijie Village in Qiongzhong, Hongkan Waterfall Scenic Area in Baisha and Hongdoupo Egret Park in Tunchang.

The integration of tourism resources has been carried out according to the principles of gradient propulsion, market orientation and participation of locals, and has reinforced cultural tourism.

According to the plan, the Department of Culture and Sports in Hainan Province has visited the central areas to explore and understand the local ethnic culture, folk customs and traditional skills of the Li and Miao nationalities, including traditional architectures, costumes, religions, arts, food and medicines, and have introduced some new sports events, as well as promote mountain sport tourism in order to support the construction of Wuzhishan National Physical Training Center and Tunchang Musehu Mountain Bike Cycling Park. This further promotes the social influence of mountain sports tourism in central part of Hainan.

Notes:

1. The majority of people who live in these areas are the Li and Miao nationalities, where tourists can visit the unique boat-shape houses built by the Li people, enjoy the local dishes such as the bamboo rice, the shanlan rice wine, or observe the local festivals.

生活在这些地区的大部分人都是黎族人和苗族人，在这里游客可以参观黎族人建造的独特船形屋，享用当地的菜肴，如竹筒饭、山兰米酒等或体验当地的节日。

2. The Department of Culture and Sports of Hainan Province announced on August 21st, 2015 that Hainan Province has planned to integrate resources in Baoting, Baisha, Qiongzhong, Wuzhishan, Tunchang and Ding' an to build a central cultural tourism green belt involving ecological culture, culture of Li and Miao nationalities, mountain sports and rural culture, so as to promote the integration and development of central cultural tourism.

海南省文体厅于 2015 年 8 月 21 日宣布，海南省计划整合资源，在保亭、白沙、琼中、五指山、屯昌、定安打造中部文化旅游绿化带，涵盖生态文化，苗族、黎族文化，山地运动和乡村文化，促进中部文化旅游整合发展。

3. There are 22 ecological and cultural scenic areas under construction or

expansion, including Maogan Ecological Tourism Area in Baoting, Butterfly Ecological Gardens in Wuzhishan, cliff inscriptions cluster in Shijie Village in Qiongzhong, Hongkan Waterfall Scenic Area in Baisha and Hongdoupo Egret Park in Tunchang.

有 22 个生态文化景区正在建设或扩建中，其中包括保亭毛感生态旅游区、五指山蝴蝶生态园、琼中仕阶村摩崖石刻群、白沙红坎瀑布风景区和屯昌洪斗坡白鹭公园。

4. The integration of tourism resources has been carried out according to the principles of gradient propulsion, market orientation and participation of locals, and has reinforced cultural tourism.

旅游资源整合按照梯度推进、市场定位和当地人参与的原则进行，加强文化旅游。

5. According to the plan, the Department of Culture and Sports in Hainan Province has visited the central areas to explore and understand the local ethnic culture, folk customs and traditional skills of the Li and Miao nationalities, including traditional architectures, costumes, religions, arts, food and medicines, and have introduced some new sports events, as well as promote mountain sport tourism in order to support the construction of Wuzhishan National Physical Training Center and Tunchang Musehu Mountain Bike Cycling Park.

根据规划，海南省文体厅到访中部地区探索和了解当地的民族文化、民俗风情、黎、苗族传统技能，包括传统建筑、服饰、宗教、艺术、美食和药品。为了支持五指山国家体育训练基地和屯昌木色湖山地自行车公园建设，还出台一些新的体育赛事，促进山地体育旅游。

Chapter 2　Tunchang

Tunchang is located in central Hainan. It borders Ding' an and Qionghai in the east, Qiongzhong in the south, Chengmai in the northwest, and it is 85 kilometers away from Haikou. It is situated on the Haiyu Central Highway, at the foot of Wuzhi Mountain. Tunchang is a typically hilly area, with mountainous land accounting for 5% and hills for 85% of the county .

Yangjiaoling Crystal Mine

Yangjiaoling Crystal Mine is one of the most famous crystal mines in China. Crystal from Hainan is of high quality. It is recorded that Chairman Mao' s coffin in Beijing was made from Tunchang Yangjiaoling crystal.

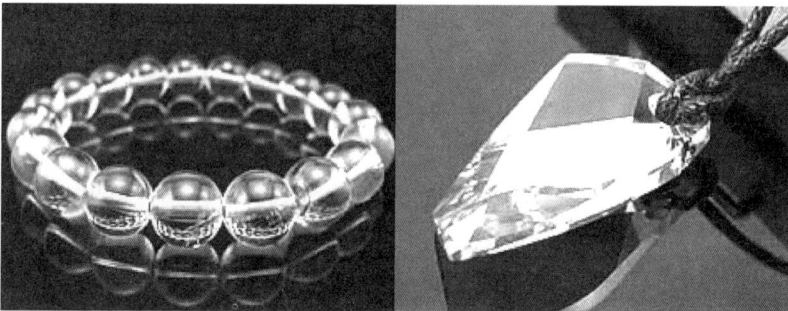

The crystal products look pure and shiny. Necklaces, bracelets, earrings, glasses and other crystal ornaments are not only decorative, but also good to people' s health. There are some DIY shops available to use your imagination and create your own unique gifts.

Wolong Hill

Wolong Hill, 499 meters high, is a peaceful scenic spot located 11 kilometers to the north of Tunchang. It is named "Wolong", which literally means a lying dragon, because the hill looks like a lying dragon. On the hill, visitors can enjoy twelve unique scenic spots.

At the foot of the hill is a beautiful old glacial lake—Long Lake, which is about to be developed into an eco-tourism center as part of Hainan's green, clean and sustainable tourism development. Just bring some food and water, and enjoy the peaceful nature.

Fengmu Deer Farm

Built in 1963, Fengmu Deer Farm is the biggest farm of this kind in Hainan. It is located in the southeast of Tunchang, 27 kilometers from Tuncheng Town. It is constructed on a small peninsula by a small lake. There are over 700 deers raised in the farm and classified into different groups namely David's Deer, Eld's Deer, Red Deer, and Spotted Deer. For some tamed deers, visitors may take pictures with them.

Over 40 years' breeding experience, the farm has produced more than 30 kinds of deer products such as: deer wine, deer tonic, deer medicine and venison. In 1997, this farm was rewarded as National Excellent Demonstration Farm. With luxuriant greenery, the farm offers perfect environment for deer breeding.

Notes:

1. It is recorded that Chairman Mao's coffin in Beijing was made from Tunchang Yangjiaoling crystal.

据载毛主席的水晶棺就是用屯昌羊角岭水晶石制成的。

2. Necklaces, bracelets, earrings, glasses and other crystal ornaments are not

only decorative, but also good to people's health.

项链、手镯、耳环、眼镜等水晶饰品不仅具有装饰性，而且有益于健康。

3. It is named "Wolong", which literally means a lying dragon, because the hill looks like a lying dragon.

它的名字叫"卧龙"，意思是一条躺着的龙，因为这座山看起来像一条躺着的龙。

4. At the foot of the hill is a beautiful old glacial lake—Long Lake, which is about to be developed into an eco-tourism center as a part of Hainan's green, clean and sustainable tourism development.

山脚下是一个美丽的冰湖——龙湖，它将很快发展成生态旅游中心，成为海南绿色、清洁和可持续旅游业发展的一部分。

5. There are over 700 deers raised in the farm and classified into different groups namely David's Deer, Eld's Deer, Red Deer, and Spotted Deer.

农场饲养的鹿有 700 多只，分别为麋鹿、坡鹿、马鹿和梅花鹿等不同种类。

Chapter 3 Qiongzhong Li and Miao Autonomous County

Qiongzhong Li and Miao Autonomous County is located in the center of Hainan Island and the north side of Wuzhi Mountain. There are a few Chinese expressions often used to describe the area's reputation in Hainan Province, including "headstream of the three rivers" "forest kingdom" "home of green oranges", and "homeland of the Li and Miao ethnic groups".

The County's name "Qiongzhong" means the center of Hainan Island. In the Ming and Qing Dynasties, Qiongzhong belonged to Ding'an. In February 1948, the Qiongya Communist established Qiongzhong County and it was under the jurisdiction of the Qiongya Eastern Prefecture. In March 1949, it was incorporated into the Administrative Committee of Qiongya minority autonomous regions.

On November 20th, 1987, the State Council approved the revocation of Qiongzhong County and established Qiongzhong Li and Miao Autonomous County and it was placed under the jurisdiction of the Hainan administrative region. In April 1988 Hainan Province was established. Then Qiongzhong Li and Miao Autonomous County was under the jurisdiction of Hainan Province directly.

Qiongzhong County is located in tropical marine monsoon climate zone. Surrounded by hills, the climate is mild with abundant rainfall. The annual average temperature is

22 ℃. The annual average sunshine time is 1,600 ~ 2,000 hours. The annual average relative humidity is 80% ~ 85%.

Qiongzhong possesses large expanses of virgin rainforest, a laid-back rural environment, the ancient cultures of the Li and Miao ethnic groups, and a unique traditional cultural community. More and more people are drawn to Qiongzhong every year for its charm and beauty.

Baihua Ridge Tourism Zone

Baihua Ridge Tourism Zone is situated seven kilometers southeast of Genying Town of Qiongzhong. It is a "natural greenhouse" and one of Hainan Province's most treasured nature preserves. The tourism zone features natural landscapes of virgin forest, rare and precious animals and plants, hot spring and waterfalls.

Baihua Ridge is as high as 1,100 meters at the peak. It has various kinds of plants and spectacular water landscapes. Baihua Ridge Waterfall is the most significant scenery in the zone with a drop of 300 meters, making a thunderous noise.

In addition to the above mentioned, Baihua Ridge also enables visitors to view ancient banyan trees in their natural surroundings.

Limu Mountain National Forest Park

About 165 kilometers away from Haikou, Limu Mountain National Forest Park is situated in Qiongzhong. With the highest altitude of 1,411 meters, it covers an area of 12,900 hectares, among which natural forest accounts for 7,300 hectares. As a tropical rainforest, it is rich in tropical biological resources including more than 2,000 kinds of plants and 58 kinds of rare or endangered wild animals.

Limu Mountain is a sacred place for the Li nationality, the earliest inhabitants of Hainan Province, who still retain a simple lifestyle with unique traditional customs. As one of the three great mountains in Hainan, Limu Mountain features a lot of waterfalls. It is one of the most scenic parks in all of Hainan, featuring rugged mountains and vast woodlands, which is the traditional home of the Li people. It is a rich mixture of tropical and subtropical forests, spectacular views and relaxing surroundings.

Limu Mountain National Forest Park consists of five areas: Yinggeling, Jinxiugu, Tianhe, Diaodengling and Limushi. Each area is basically covered with virgin forest. In addition, it is the source of three great rivers in Hainan: Nandu, Wanquan and Changhua. Every morning thousands of brooks leap down the mountainside from an altitude of more than 1,000 meters, which is quite spectacular.

The climate in Limu Mountain is very pleasant with an average temperature of 22.5℃. It is a popular place for adventurers and tourists. With a number of great trails for hikes Limu Mountain is one of the most fulfilling locations in Hainan. It is advisable to climb the mountain from the administration office in Limu Mountain National Forest Park, which is about 16 kilometers from the park gate. Hiring a guide while climbing is a better choice, for there are many forks in the trail and it is easy to get lost in the forest. For the areas with clear indication, a guide is not a must.

Bamboo-tube-cooked Rice

Bamboo-tube-cooked Rice is a featured snack for Li people. It is usually made when the people go out far, climb the mountain to hunt or treat guests. The cooking procedure is a little bit complex. Use the fragrant Shanlan Rice which is a kind of unique rice in Qiongzhong to go together with the meat as raw material, put them into fresh bamboo, add the right amount of water, then use the leaf of banana to block it up, finally burn the green bamboo on the fire. Currently, in the guest houses and the tour villages of Li Clan, we can taste the fragrant bamboo rice. It is very nice to eat bamboo rice, while drinking

Shanlan Wine which is made by the local Li people.

Qiongzhong Green Oranges

Green oranges from Qiongzhong County are rather unique. They ripen faster than others of their kind, so they have a very competitive strength on the market. They have become known nationally because of their thin green peel, sweet taste, and abundance of juice. In comparison to other oranges, their fibers are finer, so the taste is better.

Recently, the local government has sustained the production of green oranges and considered it as an important project. They provide a lot of support for the traders and merchants within the industry, including sending out packaging material. They also strictly monitor the harvesting periods and the quality of the goods. What's more, online commercial platforms have been used to the fullest to promote the green oranges from Qiongzhong on the national level.

For those who enjoy the outdoors and look for organic life, there are some orchards in the village where you can pick fresh green oranges, taste its juicy meat and enjoy its rich nutrients during the months from October to December.

Notes:

1. Baihua Ridge Waterfall is the most significant scenery in the zone with a drop of 300 meters, making a thunderous noise.

百花岭瀑布是全区最重要的景观，落差 300 米，发出雷鸣般的响声。

2. Limu Mountain National Forest Park consists of five areas: Yinggeling, Jinxiugu, Tianhe, Diaodengling and Limushi.

黎母山国家森林公园主要景点由鹦哥岭景区、锦绣谷景区、天河景区、吊灯岭景区和黎母石景区五大片区组成。

3. Every morning thousands of brooks leap down the mountainside from an altitude of more than 1, 000 meters, which is quite spectacular.

清晨，在海拔 1 000 多米的地方有无数条溪流从山间跌落，极为壮观。

4. Use the fragrant Shanlan Rice which is a kind of unique rice in Qiongzhong to go together with the meat as raw material, put them into fresh bamboo, add the right amount of water, then use the leaf of banana to block it up, finally burn the green bamboo on the fire.

用琼中特有的山兰香米配肉末为原料，放进新鲜的竹筒中，加适量的水，再用香蕉叶将竹筒口堵严，在炭火中将绿竹烤焦即可。

5. For those who enjoy the outdoors and look for organic life, there are some orchards in the village where you can pick fresh green oranges, taste its juicy meat and enjoy its rich nutrients during the months from October to December.

对于那些喜欢户外活动和寻找有机生活的人来说，可以在十月到十二月期间去村里果园采摘新鲜的绿橙，品尝它多汁的果肉，获取丰富的营养。

Chapter 4　Wuzhishan

Wuzhishan City is located at the center of Hainan Island and named after the adjacent Wuzhi Mountain, the highest point of the island. The city has a total area of 1,168.9 square kilometers and a population of 106,500 according to the statistics in 2017.

Wuzhi Mountain, a legendary place frequently mentioned in Chinese classic literature, holds one of the rare virgin tropical rainforests in China, and its ecological system is abundant with endangered species of plants and animals.

Different from the humid weather and salty air in Sanya, the temperature in Wuzhishan, remains cool with green vegetation flourishing all the year round. The annual average temperature of Wuzhishan is 22.4℃. Locals say they do not have four distinct seasons, but they can experience that each day, which means it is as warm as spring in the morning, hot as summer at noon, cool as autumn in the afternoon and cold as winter at night.

Wuzhi Mountain is rich in mineral resources with high exploitation value, such as kaolin, marble, granite, graphite ore, mineral water and so on. The city's forest coverage rate is 86.4% with over 1,400 kinds of forest woody plants, 150 kinds of advanced precious wood, and 1,000 kinds of medicinal plants. Wuzhishan also boasts wide variety of animals, accounting for 22% of the total number of animals in Hainan Island. Many biological species are unique in the mountain.

The Li people are original inhabitants of Hainan Island, who have their own style of living, food, costumes, marriage and festivals. Like Li people, Miao and Hui peoples also live in the central and southern parts of the island, including Qiongzhong, Baoting, Baisha, Lingshui, Changjiang, Sanya and Wuzhishan.

Chubao Village, the only well-preserved primitive village of Li ethnic minority group, is located at the foot of Wuzhi Mountain. It is also a miniature of the life and cultural changes of Li ethnic minority. 58 households with a population of 320 in the village are all living in the rail-style building (also known as Hanging building) with special living features of Li ethnic minority, which serves as a very special case quite different from the common boat-shaped house of Li ethnic minority. The senior villagers still keep the traditional living styles of Li ethnic minority.

Wuzhi Mountain

As the highest mountain in Hainan Island, Wuzhi Mountain makes it one of the symbols of Hainan and also one of the famous mountains in China. The name of the mountain is derived from its five peaks.

The mountain ranges from southwest to northeast. The first peak of the mountain is like a huge pyramid with elevation of 1,300 meters high and the top of the peak is piercing into the sky obliquely. The second peak of the mountain is the highest peak of the Wuzhi Mountain with elevation of 1,876 meters high. Between the first peak and the second peak there is a "Sky Bridge" built with a natural huge stone. As it is surrounded with cloud and mist all the year, it is called the Fairy Bridge with a lot of mythology stories. The third peak is the

highest peak originally but its peak was cut by thunders several years ago, so it became a bit lower than before. Although these five peaks' tops are standing separately, their mountain bodies are joined together.

Looking at the Wuzhi Mountain from distance, with green forest and cloud around, these five green peaks are piercing into the sky like fingers. The scenery is beautiful and spectacular.

When tourists climb up along the mountain roads, they will find the cloud and mist gushing to them from up to down gradually. This is one of the features of the Wuzhi Mountain. If they climb to the top, the cloud and mist are much thicker as if they were in the space. Looking down, they can see the green waves are all under their eyes and water is connected with the sky. These are too beautiful to be absorbed all at once.

The main rivers and streams in Hainan Island originate from the Wuzhi Mountain. The scenery of mountain and rivers forms the beautiful landscape. On the mountain there is spacious original forest. The falling leaves are as thick as 50 centimeters. A kind of unique fragrance is full of air, so some biologists and botanists say that Wuzhi Mountain is the green treasure hidden among many trees for hundreds of years.

Meanwhile Wuzhi Mountain is also the kingdom of precious animals and birds, such as reptiles, birds and animals. When visitors travel Wuzhi Mountain, they will see animals coming out to look for food or playing with each other now and then.

A good time to visit is on the third day of the third month of the lunar calendar, when lots of Li people gather for an annual festival, which is the festival for lovers.

Wuzhishan Grand Canyon Rafting

If one wants to enjoy an exciting rafting (or river drifting) experience through the rainforest of Hainan, Wuzhishan Grand Canyon is the perfect place to try.

This canyon drift follows the course of the river that meanders through the rainforest valleys around Wuzhi Mountain. The route takes about two hours.

As the 9-km-long Wuzhishan River winds through the rainforest of Wuzhi Mountain, challengers have to pass through beautiful canyons at high speeds, descending a total of 80 meters along the rafting course with the highest drops on the course measuring around 8 meters. The canyon river rafting in Wuzhi Mountain is thoroughly recommended for thrill seekers looking for a fun challenge during their holiday in Hainan.

Taipingshan Waterfall

The Taipingshan Waterfall, situated on an 800-meter-high cliff on Taiping Mountain, is one of the top attractions in the Taiping Mountain area. The rocks found there are seen from tier upon tier. The water which comes from the lake on top of the Taiping Mountain, splashes on the rock down to steep cliff making thunderous sounds. The water streams down

the rock into a big rocky pool, which forms the second waterfall and then pours down another steep cliff, forming the third deep pool.

During the summer, the Taipingshan Waterfall is one of the most popular tourist destinations in the region. On the west of the waterfall there is a waterfall-watching pavilion. When visiting here the splashing view of the fall creates a fantasy world of water.

Yahu Terrace Field

Yahu Terrace Field in Wuzhishan offers breathtaking terraced vistas unlike any other area of Hainan.

Located within Maoyang Township, 40 kilometers away from Wuzhishan, a vast region of terraces stretches layer upon layer along the slopes, from mountain tops to the borders of verdant forests. This is the Yahu Terrace Field which covers an area of about 1,100 acres.

Although few tourists visit the terraces, photographers love the thrilling beauty of the landscape. The beautiful natural landscape of Yahu Terrace Field can be explored in every season. Rain water and springs from mountains flow down to the terraces and the whole cycle repeats itself perpetually.

In spring, the fields are irrigated with spring water from the forest above to rejuvenate the area and the terrace looks like great mirrors hung on the hillsides in preparation for the next growing season. In summer, waves of green seem to flow down the mountainside. The theme for autumn is the harvest, when the mountainside takes on the golden color of ripened millet.

Apart from its amazing scenery, Wuzhishan is also in an area where some of Hainan's ethnic minority culture can be experienced, such as the residence of Li and Miao minorities. Tourists can join them to experience the traditional way of life and culture, visiting the traditional architecture of the Li people, whose houses resemble overturned boats. Visitors can stay with local families to enjoy Wuzhishan cuisine such as Shanlan Wine and Three-colored Rice.

Three-color Sticky Rice

Three-color Sticky Rice is a traditional food of Miao minority in Hainan. Usually, it is a special snack only served during the March 3rd festivals. The three colors are respectively yellow, black, and red. When served side by side, it really looks appealing. The colors are made from local vegetation, making this colorful and tasty dish an excellent vegetarian option.

Notes:

1. Wuzhi Mountain is rich in mineral resources with high exploitation value, such as kaolin, marble, granite, graphite ore, mineral water and so on.

五指山具有丰富的矿产资源，具有很高的开发利用价值，如高岭土、大理石、花岗岩、石墨矿、矿泉水等。

2. Like Li people, Miao and Hui peoples also live in the central and southern parts of the island, including Qiongzhong, Baoting, Baisha, Lingshui, Changjiang, Sanya and Wuzhishan.

就像黎族人一样，大部分苗、回族人民生活在海南岛的中部和南部地区，包括琼中、保亭、白沙、陵水、昌江、三亚和五指山。

3. Between the first peak and the second peak there is a "Sky Bridge" built with a natural huge stone.

在第一高峰和第二高峰之间，有一座天然巨石形成的"空中大桥"。

4. When tourists climb up along the mountain roads, they will find the cloud and mist gushing to them from up to down gradually.

当游客们沿着山路攀爬时，会发现云雾自上而下逐渐向他们涌来。

5. In spring, the fields are irrigated with spring water from the forest above to rejuvenate the area and the terrace looks like great mirrors hung on the hillsides in preparation for the next growing season.

春天引水灌溉的时候，水满田畴，梯田犹如镶嵌在群山之间的一块块明镜，为生长季节做准备。

Chapter 5   Baoting Li and Miao Autonomous County

Baoting Li and Miao Autonomous County, located at the foot of Wuzhi Mountain in the south of Hainan Island, covers a total area of 1,166.6 kilometers. It is one of the few autonomous counties to win national awards such as "National Clean County" "National Garden County" "National Cultural County", and "National Traditional Art County". Li and Miao minorities account for 60% of population of the whole county. The traditional culture prevails here and there.

Local crafts such as Li brocades, quilts made from tree bark, and traditional bamboo musical instruments have been listed of National Intangible Cultural Heritage Protection. Baoting has the most protected cultural heritage items of all cities and areas in Hainan.

Baoting enjoys a warm climate with an annual average temperature of 23℃. Forest covers 85.2% of the county's area, including Hainan's most unspoiled rainforest. Hot springs, rock caves, and traditional Hainan culture also attract tourists. Tourism resources in Baoting emphasize rain forests, hot springs, rock caves, eco-tourism, traditional culture, and rural scenery, all of which are very different from Sanya's sun, beach and sea.

Yanoda Rainforest Cultural Tourism Zone

Yanoda Rainforest Cultural Tourism Zone is famous for the unique rainforest at 18 degrees north latitude. Since it opened it has been a great boost to Hainan Island' s tourist economy.

Ya, No, and Da originally indicated the numeral words "one, two, three" in the Hainan dialect. Yanoda Rainforest Cultural Tourism Zone gives new meanings to these words: "Ya" means innovation, "No" represents promise and "Da" refers to practice. The concept of Yanoda here is to preserve the native cultures and exhibit the essence of Chinese traditional culture.

Yanoda Rainforest Cutural Tourism Zone covers a total area of 45 square kilometers encircled by an ecological protection area of 123 square kilometers. The total investment of the project amounts to about RMB 3. 9 billion.

With the investment RMB 0. 2 billion already, Yanoda has already built two scenic zones, the Rainforest Valley and the Dreamworld Valley. All spots are connected by totally 18 kilometers inner ring roads with the traffic means of American battery cars, high-class shuttle buses, plank roads alongside cliffs and suspension bridges on waterfalls. The Rainforest Valley contains six rainforest wonders such as plant strangle, flower basket, old stems blossom, great roots, intertwined vines and huge stones embraced by roots. All these natural scenes are symbolizing the essential features of the five major rainforests in Hainan Island.

In the valleys, designed artfully according to the landscape and the mountain terrain, the plank roads lead to the deep forest, the stone staircase twist up at both sides of the huge rocks, the suspension bridges sway in midair, the steel hawsers cross up to the mountain through the waterfalls. Visitors here can feel tranquility and the mystery in the deep forest, enjoy the joyfulness of playing waterfalls, and experience the pleasant surprise and the quiver of emotion on the fantastic sky bridges in Yanoda.

Binglanggu Valley

Binglanggu Valley or Hainan Li and Miao Cultural Heritage Park was built in 1998, and ranks a national 5 A-level tourist attraction. It covers an area of more than 333 hectares in total. Binglanggu attracts more than 1. 2 million tourists every year, and is a multiethnic, multicultural tourist scenic area incorporating sightseeing, cultural presentation, custom experience and entertainment. It consists of Intangible Cultural Heritage Village, Ganza Li Village and Miao Village, together with a great live musical drama about Li and Miao Culture.

Visitors may indulge in enchanting beauty of nature, appreciating folk customs, ethnic melody, enjoying ethnic foods, Li and Miao styled lodging and cultural art. Binglanggu is the only tourist area themed by primitive and ecological Li and Miao culture, and has made great contribution to exploring, saving and promoting local culture of Hainan Island. Also there are several Hainan national intangible cultural heritage items exhibited in Binglanggu, making it the best exhibition window of ethnic minority culture of Hainan Island.

A number of cultural experiences await you in these traditional villages, you can get a feel for the daily lives of the indigenous people who live here, and learn a little of the Li and Miao culture. You can also enjoy the special treat of seeing the incredible "Fire and Knife" performance of the Miao people.

Seven Fairy Mountain

As one of the famous scenic spots in Hainan Island, Seven Fairy Mountain lies in Baoting National Rainforest Park, 9 kilometers to the northeast of Baoting County. The elevation of the mountain is 1,126 meters above sea level. There are seven stones projecting to the sky on the top of the mountain, just like seven fingers pointing to the sky, so it is called Seven-finger Mountain by the local people. During noon time, the majestic statues of the stones look like seven swords as the mist is dispelled. To look from a long distance, the seven peaks look like seven beautiful ladies, standing in thin veils, so come with the name of Seven Fairy Mountain.

There are numerous waterfalls scattered in the rainforest with inhabiting little creatures such as crabs, small fish and so on. Every now and then, beautiful butterflies can be seen flying overhead. At the same time, spiders are weaving webs, and insects or birds are singing. There are small huts and stone benches placed by the locals for the visitors to have a rest. The way leading to the peak is thoroughly paved with stones. As the gradient of the mountain is about 60 degrees, so it is fenced with banister rails.

The foot of the mountain is dotted with more than twenty hot springs. Among them, seven belong to self-spray hot springs with water in the amount of 7,000 cubic meters a day. The highest temperature reaches 94℃ while the average is about 70℃. As hot spring contains rich mineral which is believe to be good for health, many people come here for hot spring bath. It is said that hot springs can cure such diseases as rheumatism, dermatosis and itchiness, etc. After the exhausting mountain climbing, it certainly can ease your ache and abate your sour legs and feet.

Li Brocade

As one of the most notable traditional handicrafts of Hainan Island, Li brocade has been listed on the National Intangible Cultural Heritage Protection.

Traditionally, the production of cloth was a basic skill for Li women, who were required to learn the whole process of spinning, weaving, dyeing and embroidery.

Regarded as a "living fossil" of Chinese textiles, the art of Li brocade is a unique folk art and textile craft in China with a long history of more than 2,500 years invented by the Li people.

These costumes are still worn by many people in the countryside on a daily basis and used for formal and ceremonial occasions. It typically takes around 3 to 4 months, or even longer, to create an entire costume.

In recent years, Baoting has greatly promoted the development of the brocade by improving the techniques, patterns and specialized software to maintain its traditions as well as to improve its quality. With the use of advanced techniques, Li brocade still maintains its traditional charm in the modern time.

Notes:

1. Local crafts such as Li brocades, quilts made from tree bark, and traditional bamboo musical instruments have been listed on the National Intangible Cultural Heritage Protection.

当地的工艺品如黎锦，树皮被子和传统竹乐器已被列入国家非物质文化遗产保护名录。

2. It consists of Intangible Cultural Heritage Village, Ganza Li Village and Miao Village, together with a great live musical drama about Li and Miao Culture.

景区由非物质文化遗产村、甘什黎村、雨林苗寨，以及大型黎苗文化实景演出组成。

3. To look from a long distance, the seven peaks look like seven beautiful ladies, standing in thin veils, so come with the name of Seven Fairy Mountain.

从远处看，七峰像七个美女，蒙着薄纱站在那儿，这就是七仙岭名字的由来。

4. Traditionally, the production of cloth was a basic skill for Li women, who were required to learn the whole process of spinning, weaving, dyeing and embroidery.

从传统上讲，织布是黎族妇女的基本技能，她们需要学习纺纱、织布、染色和刺绣的全过程。

5. Regarded as a "living fossil" of Chinese textiles, the art of Li brocade is a unique folk art and textile craft in China with a long history of more than 2,500 years invented by the Li people.

黎锦艺术被誉为中国纺织品的"活化石"，是黎族人民发明的具有 2 500 多年历史的中国独特的民间艺术和纺织工艺。

References

［1］尼葛洛·庞帝. 数字化生存［M］. 胡泳，等，译. 海口：海南出版社，1997.

［2］曹阳，孙博. 海南模拟导游［M］. 上海：复旦大学出版社，2010.

［3］陈大坚，李旭芳. 模拟导游［M］. 海口：南海出版公司，2002.

［4］陈耀. 海南旅游概览［M］. 海口：南海出版公司，2004.

［5］纪俊超. 英语海南导游［M］. 北京：中国旅游出版社，2009.

［6］卿志军. 旅游文化传播学［M］. 成都：四川大学出版社，2008.

［7］龙晓苑. 数字化艺术［M］. 北京：北京大学出版社，2001.

［8］潘文焰. 旅游文化与传播［M］. 北京：北京大学出版社，2011.

［9］庞守明. 精编海南导游词［M］. 北京：中国旅游出版社，2007.

［10］《尚游手册》编委会. 海南旅图［M］. 北京：星球地图出版社，2011.

［11］赵建国，王大钟. 旅游传播论［M］. 北京：中国社会科学出版社，2011.

［12］张伯敏. 海南实用旅游英语［M］. 北京：中国人民大学出版社，2012.

［13］邹本涛，谢春山. 旅游文化学［M］. 北京：中国旅游出版社，2008.

［14］http：//en. haikoutour. gov. cn/view. asp？ArticleID＝81.

［15］http：//travel. china. com/vane/featured/hainan_ en/11168101/20141118/18978441_ all. html.

［16］http：//www. chinatravel. com/hainan/transport. htm.

［17］http：//www. cots. com. cn/english/City/HaiNanSheng. html.

［18］http：//www. china-10. com/brand/5235. html.

[19] http: //www. mlairport. com/autoweb/autoweb/secondpage/hkml _ ldmshkml _ jb. html.

[20] http: //www. hainan. gov. cn/zxtadata-7112. html.

[21] https: //defence. pk/pdf/threads/from-may-1st-59-nationals-can-enter-chinas-hainan-for-travel-without-visas-for-30-days. 554236/.

[22] http: //www. chinatoptours. com/Guide/guidecontent/Haikou-Introduction. html.

[23] http: //en. haikoutour. gov. cn.

[24] http: //www. chinatravelpage. com/qilou-old-street-in-haikou-a-historical-and-cultural-block-of-china.

[25] http: //www. chinatoptours. com/Guide/guidecontent/Hairui-Tomb. html.

[26] http: //www. movietownhaikou. com/en-us/introduction. php.

[27] http: //www. sanyaweb. com/sight _ qionghai _ wanquan _ river _ tourism _ zone. html.

[28] http: //www. whatsonsanya. com/sanya-wine-2217. html.

[29] http: //www. binglanggu. com/index. php? sn = en_ index.

[30] http: //www. sunnysanya. com/Things_ Do_ Sanya_ Hainan_ Island/The_ Legend_ of_ Romance_ Show_ Sanya_ Hainan_ Island. asp.

[31] http: //en. aitianya. cn/page_ dd. php? xuh =265.

[32] http: //en. sanyapark. com/.

[33] http: //www. xian-tours. cn/China-Attractions/Sanya-Attractions/LuhuitouPark-Attractions. Html.

[34] http: //www. 898. travel/page_ en. php? xuh =8847.

[35] http: //travel. china. com/vane/featured/hainan_ en/11168101/20141119/18982332_ all. html# page_ 2.

[36] http: //www. travelchinaguide. com/attraction/hainan/haikou/wuzhi-mountain. htm.

[37] http: //www. whatsonsanya. com/sanya-travel-2842. html.

[38] http: //dongshanling. net/en/history. php.

［39］ http：//www. whatsonsanya. com/sanya-travel-2807. html.

［40］ http：//en. visithainan. gov. cn/English/FoodParadise/LocalSpecialties/ Wenchangs/.

［41］ http：//www. globalsanya. com/htel/newshtml/WhatsNew/20140217142327. asp.

［42］ http：//travel. china. com/vane/featured/hainan_ en/11168101/20141119/ 18982332. html.

［43］ http：//www. hi. chinanews. com/hnnew/2014-10-29/4_ 38927. html.

［44］ http：//english. boaoforum. org/gylten/index. jhtml.

［45］ http：//www. sanyatravelguide. com/sightseeingview. asp？ SightID = 22.

［46］ http：//en. visithainan. gov. cn/English/FoodParadise/LocalSpecialties/ Qionghais/201412/t20141201_ 54016. html.

［47］ http：//www. qionghai. gov. cn/read. jsp？ id = 81197.

［48］ http：//baijiahao. baidu. com/s？ id = 1560374045022732&wfr = spider& for = pc.

［49］ http：//en. hainan. gov. cn/englishgov/map/danzhou/ScenicSpot/200912/ t20091215_ 38607. html.

［50］ http：//www. danzhou. gov. cn/dzgov/dzyw/Glimpse/201509/t20150917_ 1666865. html.

［51］ http：//www. danzhou. gov. cn/dzgov/ywdt/jrdz/201709/t20170922_ 2430570. html.